Charles Hall,
from. Rivers Bosanquet,
25-12-68.

A LIFE APART

BY THE SAME AUTHOR:

THE FUGITIVES

THE MASK AND THE MAN

THE GOVERNOR

THE DIRECTOR

THE SURGEON

THE JUDGE

A LIFE APART

by

ALAN THOMAS

LONDON
VICTOR GOLLANCZ LTD
1968

575 00082 1

MADE AND PRINTED IN GREAT BRITAIN BY
THE GARDEN CITY PRESS LIMITED
LETCHWORTH, HERTFORDSHIRE

CONTENTS

PART ONE: *Growing Up*   9

PART TWO: '*The Great Adventure*'   31

PART THREE: *In Memoriam*   75

PART ONE

GROWING UP

I

Nₒₜ ᵦₑᵢₙg ₒբ a heroic turn I was more than a little embarrassed when at the age of eleven, contrary to all expectation and good sense, I found myself hailed as a hero.

We were at prep. In front of me sat a boy wearing an enormous Eton collar, spotless and inviting. Having a pen in my hand I dipped it in the ink and carefully traced the boy's name and initial along the lower edge of the collar—J. Barham. The surface, I was interested to see, took the ink well. The letters, a shade too small perhaps, were more or less neatly printed and the general effect was pleasing. The writing relieved the collar's whiteness.

I spent a moment contemplating my handiwork with satisfaction and then returned to my prep. At the end of the period I had completely forgotten the writing on the collar and I passed an untroubled night.

I must explain that the classrooms in which we sat gave off on to a long corridor and traffic in the corridor was clearly audible. It was customary for any important notice which had not been given out at roll-call in the morning to be communicated to the school by the headmaster who would himself visit each classroom for the purpose. When this happened, you knew of it in advance, because you could hear the door of each room in turn being opened and shut, and, in the intervals, the steps of the headmaster coming nearer.

So it was on the following morning. I was sitting in the fourth classroom. The doors of the other three rooms had been opened and shut and we knew that something was being 'given out'. We heard the headmaster's footsteps approaching our room. I was interested, as we all were, in the forthcoming notice, whatever it might be, mainly because it broke into the lesson and gave us something else to think about. It never occurred to me that I would be in any way involved.

The footfalls drew near to our room and the door opened. The headmaster appeared. In his hand he was carrying—a collar.

'Someone,' he announced, holding the collar up for all to see, 'has defaced this collar by scribbling on it. I want the boy who did it to own up.'

At King Alfred School, where I had just spent five happy years, no one had ever thought of concealing an action. If you had done wrong, your action was voted upon. An adverse vote was the worst punishment that could befall you. (K.A.S. was a co-educational establishment, regarded in those days as 'advanced'.)

Involuntarily my hand shot up.

'I did it,' I said.

Mr. Stallard, the headmaster, was clearly surprised. All he said for the moment was 'Oh!'

I waited. I had the feeling that there and then he would inaugurate a discussion on the subject, as my previous headmaster would have done. I should have been invited to give an explanation and after that the class would have expressed its view.

I was mistaken. After a pause Mr. Stallard said: 'You will come to my study immediately after lunch.'

The rest of the morning I spent in an agony of suspense. When the class was over several boys told me I was 'for it'. Speculation ranged round 'the bat' or the cane. The bat, it appeared, was used for minor offences: the cane for more serious cases. In my case general opinion favoured the cane.

For the first time in my life I experienced deep fear. Never before had I been beaten. Yet, even more than the cane (which would be bad enough) I feared the dark horror with which the prospect of the punishment surrounded me. What sort of place had I been sent to? What jungle was I walking in?

Shivering with fear, I retired to the lavatory—and prayed. I asked Jesus to forgive me for what I had done and to soften Mr. Stallard's heart.

After that I felt a little better, and was able to eat lunch.

When the meal was over but before we were allowed to go, Mr. Stallard got up and called for silence. I had no idea what he was going to talk about. All I hoped was that he would make it short so that my suspense would be the sooner over.

'An event occurred this morning,' he began, 'to which I wish to draw the school's attention. Last night a boy had his collar scribbled on—' My heart gave a thump. I wished that I were dead.

'It was a nasty thing to do,' he continued, pronouncing the word 'nasty' with a short 'a', 'the sort of thing that street urchins do—only they scribble on walls. Also it ruined the collar. When the thing was brought to my notice this morning, I wondered how I was going to discover the culprit, seeing that there was no evidence to show where the blame was to be fixed. Accordingly I did the only thing I could do. I went round the school, asking for the boy who did this thing to own up. I wondered whether I was going to be disappointed. I hoped I would not be, because I have always considered this to be a school for gentlemen.' Mr. Stallard paused a moment to let this impressive thought sink in. 'I am glad to say, gentlemen, that I was not disappointed. Hardly had I asked the question in the room where the culprit was sitting than up went his hand and the words came out: "I did it, sir." The boy who did it and who owned up to doing it was Thomas.'

At this point the school broke into loud applause.

'Stop clapping!' commanded Mr. Stallard sternly, feeling no doubt that the picture was getting out of perspective. 'This is not a subject for applause. Thomas had no business to go scribbling on collars and in doing what he did afterwards, that is to say in owning up, he only did what I hope every other boy in the school would have done—'

Again and in spite of Mr. Stallard's order the school broke out in applause, the boy next to me thumping me enthusiastically on the back.

The headmaster held up his hand for order and after reproving the school a second time for clapping, observed as ominously as he could that Thomas was due to meet him in his study afterwards. This remark, however, which was intended to be damping, did not dim my temporary popularity. From the remarks that were made to me by other boys it was clear that whatever might happen to me in the study afterwards I carried with me the good wishes of my fellows.

So, for the first and only time during the whole of my school career, I was a hero. But my position, attained by not wholly creditable means, brought me little comfort. I felt like the king I had read about in my history book—the king who had waded to the throne through seas of blood.

The interview in the study after lunch was short. Because I had owned up I was let off the beating I was told I deserved. All that happened was that I had to pay for the collar. It cost, I think, a shilling.

II

My triumph, such as it was, did not last long. Nor was I sorry. To be known as 'the boy who owned up' was not to enjoy an enviable reputation. The truth was that I had other qualities which appeared to mark me out not so much as a hero as a butt, which caused me to be regarded as 'a character'. For one thing I started by treating the masters as we had treated them at K.A.S., that is, with the familiarity of friendship. When in my first week it became clear that I had been placed in too high a form the form-master looked at me in some astonishment.

'D'you mean to say,' quoth he, 'that this is the first time you've ever done Latin.'

'Yes,' I replied.

'And how old are you?'

'Eleven,' said I.

The tone of my answers, if not deferential, was not cheeky. I replied in a straightforward manner, feeling I had nothing to be ashamed of.

One or two of the boys tittered—which may have nettled the master.

'Don't you normally say "sir" when you speak to a master?' he enquired tartly.

This time it was my turn to be astonished.

'No,' I replied in genuine surprise, looking him straight in the face.

This brought the house down. The whole class roared with laughter. Even the master himself smiled. He saw, I think, that I had not meant to be impertinent. I was merely a freak. In a short time I would be moulded to their ways.

Then, too, I caused amusement by pronouncing Latin words as though they were French. French after all was the only other foreign language I had learnt and I assumed that Latin, being a foreign language, should be pronounced in the same way. Consequently when I said the word 'omnibus' as a Frenchman would have said it (except that I did not sound the final 's') the form shrieked with delight. They said that I was 'priceless' and wondered how on earth I thought of such jokes.

My fondness for asking questions also added to my reputation as a freak. When, in the history class, I asked why a certain historical character had acted in such a way and not otherwise, the answer from the history master came pat: 'My boy, it's no good asking me. I wasn't there.' Which at all events was an honest reply. The same master used to 'hear' us our scripture repetition (each term we had to learn a chapter of the Bible by heart). In trying to commit Romans viii to memory I came across a passage which did not seem to me to make sense: so I asked what it meant. 'My boy,' replied old Mr. Summers, 'my business is to *hear* you this chapter, not to explain it.' This perhaps was just as well, because Romans viii would have needed a good deal of explanation for boys of eleven.

My reputation for freakishness however—as for heroism— quickly evaporated: for I soon accustomed myself to the ways of the school. I did this, not because I accepted their ways as natural and sensible, but because I could not bear the consequences of being different from others. At K.A.S. individual differences had been encouraged: here they were strongly discouraged. In any case I had enough to put up with in the way of homesickness, weakness at games (though I was always fond of cricket), shyness and slowness in making friends, without wishing to be a byword in the school for freakishness. Consequently I aimed at conforming as closely as possible to everything that was 'done' and avoiding anything that savoured of originality in deed or word.

In this chameleon-like effort I succeeded. In my report at the end of my first term the headmaster wrote that after rather an unusual start I was settling down quite well.

III

The process of moulding me into the right shape under the vigilant eye of Mr. Stallard and his masters continued for three years.

As it happened I was still at Stallard's when King Edward VII died—an event with which it would have been little short of lese-majesty not to be concerned. During the days immediately before his death frequent bulletins were posted on the school notice board, and every morning at roll-call Mr. Stallard gave us the latest news of the King's health and offered special prayers on his behalf. When the end was near, Mr. Stallard came round the classrooms and made a special announcement. Poking his head inside each room he said in a voice of the utmost gravity: 'Gentlemen, the King is sinking.' Mr. Ryves, the sixth-form master, in whose class I was sitting, received this news with such apparent calm that Mr. Stallard seemed to doubt his loyalty. 'Mr. Ryves!' he repeated sternly, 'I said that the King is sinking.' Whereupon Mr. Ryves, at a loss for the right answer, rose in his place. Taking our cue from him we all stood up. This procedure appearing to satisfy Mr. Stallard, he departed. Without comment from Mr. Ryves we resumed our work.

In the course of my last week at school I was summoned to the study for what was known as 'the leaving pi-jaw' from Mr. Stallard. The object of his interview, as we all knew, was that we should have the facts of life explained to us. My knowledge of this subject was not extensive and I was interested in the headmaster's lucid account of the generative process. Having dealt with the substantial business, he went on to warn me of two dangers to be avoided 'as you would the plague'. The first related to women who 'though you will find it difficult to believe, make a habit of selling their bodies for profit'. I was not quite sure what this meant. I pictured women selling themselves for slaves—dark-skinned women, with gold rings round their arms. Where, I wondered, did this take place? Not, I hoped, on British territory, because I knew that slavery had been abolished wherever the Union Jack flew. Mr. Stallard must have noticed my perplexity. 'In the streets of London,' he went on sombrely, 'women vaunt themselves for sale. They are godless creatures, who have no sense of right or wrong. I trust that you may never, *never* fall a victim to them.' He had not, I considered, entirely cleared up the point for me. But seeing that I was expected to give some assurance on the point, I coughed and said 'No, sir,' as firmly as I could.

'The other danger,' continued Mr. Stallard, 'may be nearer at hand.' This sounded more interesting and I could not suppress a look of eagerness, which I think he must have misinterpreted : for he frowned and his voice dropped two whole tones. 'There are certain boys,' he said, 'whose lusts prompt them to unnatural vice.' I was far from understanding the meaning of this, but the phrase sounded so ominous that my heartbeats quickened. 'An older boy will take a younger boy,' went on Mr. Stallard, 'and treat him as though he were a woman.' It was my turn to frown. I did so in genuine perplexity. 'He will, as I say,' said Mr. Stallard, adding nothing by way of explanation, 'treat him as a woman.' Perhaps he had judged that I was already familiar enough with the process to require no details : at all events he offered none. 'If ever you are confronted with this crime,' he concluded, 'strike : and strike hard !' His voice here became almost savage. 'Use anything that is to hand. A boy who went forth from this school once used a water-jug and broke it over the criminal's head. I honour him for it. I hope that in like circumstances you would do the same.'

Thinking it over afterwards I found myself hoping that in my case a less unwieldy and less dangerous weapon than a water-jug would be available. I also doubted my own courage in the matter. After all, one might every easily kill someone with a water-jug—and what then? Would a reference back to Mr. Stallard be a good defence? It might be, but I felt there was a risk about it.

In giving these pi-jaws Mr. Stallard was moved by the highest motives. He pictured himself, I have no doubt, as fastening on us the armour of God. All the same the result in my case was that I came away from the talk with an unhealthy fear of sex and perhaps some curiosity about it : but with very little understanding of the subject.

IV

There had never been any question but that I should go to a public school. I myself had raised a protest. Why, I asked my parents, couldn't I continue my education at home with a private tutor, or failing that, at a day-school? I was, I argued, a misfit at a boarding-school. I was one of those boys who required regular contact with his family. Being unhappy at boarding-school how could I do my work properly? How, indeed, could I do any good at all?

My arguments, such as they were, convinced no one. I had, as it happened, taken a scholarship for Malvern. The question was settled.

One thought comforted me. Howard Hill, who had been my friend at Stallard's, was also going to Malvern. Hill and I differed in many respects. He took life cheerfully and did not know what it meant to be unpopular. I, on the other hand, always looked on the gloomy side and never mixed easily with other boys. Hill was athletic in build, an excellent boxer and generally good at games. I was short and podgy, loathed boxing and, though I was keen on cricket, never showed much promise at that game or indeed at any other. In class, if Hill's light shone rather less brilliantly, he never allowed the fact to prey on his mind. I, on the other hand, worried incessantly about my work and got through it by plodding—unlike the clever ones who knew all about a Greek unseen at a glance. Still, in my own way and in my own time, I did manage to keep up. Consequently in Hill's eyes I was something of a genius. The fact was that our friendship was compounded of admiration of each other's differing qualities. That it was sometimes strained was not unnatural, since on each side the admiration must have been mingled with some jealousy. But besides knowing Hill at school, I knew him at home—an additional bond.

At Malvern Hill and I both went to Lyon's house. The first thing I heard about it was that in the previous term there had been a purge. A number of boys had been expelled for the sin of which Mr. Stallard had warned me and, as somebody put it, the house was turning over a new leaf. All the same, when I went to bed on the first evening, I took a look at the water-jug in my cubicle. It seemed a hefty piece. I hoped that I should never have to use it. Nor did I. During my five years at Lyon's no case occurred of that particular brand of immorality. The same could not be said of other houses.

Colonel Lyon, the house-master, was a fine, upstanding figure of a man, paunchy but adroitly tailored. He had two passions and one outstanding weakness. His passions were soldiering and talking about old times. He was a colonel in the Territorials and to see him in full dress uniform taking the parade of the school O.T.C., or marching up the High Street at the head of the corps and immediately behind the band, was to watch a man fulfilling himself with enviable satisfaction. His other passion he indulged every evening when after prayers he would hold a kind of court at the foot of the stairs leading up to the cubicles. Only prefects and privileged seniors were expected to attend. Roley—as Colonel Lyon was called—would lean gracefully against the banisters and ramble on amiably to the chosen few about the good old days when he had been a boy at Malvern and in general about the glories of the past. It was a method, I suppose, of creating in us a sense of tradition and strengthening resistance to change. When in later years I was admitted to the circle I did my best to help with the prompting (Roley always liked and expected a prompt now and then: it showed you were interested). But I never became enthusiastic either about Roley's past or, for the matter of that, about the school's traditions.

Roley's weakness lay in his incapacity for what he called 'book learning'. Here, to do him justice, he made no exaggerated claims. He took the lowest form in the school and made no secret of the fact that if there had been an even lower form, the work would still have been above him. Nor did his incapacity worry him at all. The popularity it gained him was ample compensation.

As for the study and shaping of characters, Roley took all that for granted. If you were the kind of boy who fitted easily into the life of a public school, if your outlook was normal and you were good at games and took your work as it came without worrying (although Roley liked a scholar or two in his house, just to keep that end of the show going), if in short you were the kind of boy that Roley took you for—that was the proof; he was clearly turning you out a good scout.

But if you were constituted otherwise and were a misfit, Roley had no use for you. He didn't persecute you (he was far too good-natured and easy-going to persecute anyone: he left that job to the prefects) but equally he did not give you a leg up. All he did, provided you gave no trouble, was to ignore you. To parents who asked him how their son was getting on, he would reply that the boy was 'finding his feet'. So far as the boy was concerned, the quicker he found them the better.

V

New boys at Lyon's all occupied the same study. No matter how many new boys there were—two or a dozen—the same space served them all. The room, which measured about twelve by eight, had two windows: one which gave on to the inner passage, so that other boys, particularly prefects, could peer in and see what the 'new bugs' were up to. The other commanded a good view of the house lavatories. These conveniences were, so to say, public and as the common flushing system worked only at intervals, the window of our study had to be kept permanently shut. It was in fact nailed up.

My father and mother when they saw my 'study' were so upset that they complained to Roley and insisted that I should be given another study. And so I was—but at what a cost! I think if they had known how the other boys would take it out of me, they would have thought again before insisting on the move.

One compensation there was. My transfer to another study gave me a new friend. Charles Jeffries was senior to me at Malvern by a year and now, over fifty years later, I think of him still as my senior by a year. He was a fine scholar, an ace at English essays (which I could never manage) as well as being a most congenial companion. Without his help and encouragement I should never have been able to make my way to the senior classical forms at Malvern.

At the beginning of my third term I entered the Remove, and for the first time I came directly under the eye of the Headmaster.

The Rev. Sydney Rhodes James was a relic of the good old days of schoolmastering when the first object of education was to discipline the pupil. The instrument he used for this purpose was the fear of God. So far as his pupils were concerned the method had advantages. You knew where you were. You knew that if Jimmy said a thing he meant it. You knew that if you were caught in a breach of the rules, excuses would be useless. And you knew what a caning from Jimmy would mean, because he always kept the door of the room open while he was at it. In class you knew that sloppy preparation would immediately be discovered and that the punishment would not be pleasant. All these were advantages. The disadvantage was that under Jimmy's methods life, as one boy expressed it, was not worth living.

My first encounter with the Head occurred during my first week in the Remove. Every Tuesday morning the three top forms on the classical side—the Remove, the Lower Sixth and Upper Sixth—were taken by Jimmy for Greek Testament. A chapter was set beforehand so that you had time to prepare it and boys chosen at random would be called on to translate. As there were about fifty boys in the three forms your chances of being called more than once in any one term were pretty small. But you never knew. Jimmy took delight in catching people out and would sometimes pick on the same boy in two successive weeks.

There were two other boys in Lyon's who went to this class—Jeffries and Pethick, both in the Lower Sixth—and we prepared the lesson together. Jeffries, who was easily the best scholar among us, would construe aloud, while Pethick would check his translation against the Authorised Version. I followed as best I could. Both Jeffries and Pethick said that the betting was heavily against my being called on my first morning.

We walked up to the school and into the class. I took my place at the back of the room where the desks were on a dais, corresponding to the dais at the other end where Jimmy sat. A boy stood by the door to watch out for his arrival.

Presently he gave the signal and a hush fell on the room.

Then Jimmy stumped in.

He seemed, I thought, in a good mood. Having nodded to the class—rather like a Judge bobbing to the court—he settled

in his chair, gathered his gown about him and glanced at the
list which lay in front of him.

'First morning, new term,' he jerked out—he always spoke in
short, jerky sentences. 'Can't do better than start at the top.
Powell!'

There was a geniality in his tone which I rather liked.

Powell, head of the sixth form, got up and started translating.
His speech was slow and monotonous to listen to: but his con-
strue was faultless. After he had been going for a few minutes,
Jimmy said, 'All right' very abruptly and Powell sat down.

There was a pause, while Jimmy once again looked at his list.
I felt safe.

'Hmph,' he ejaculated presently. 'Started at the top. May as
well jump to the bottom. Thomas!'

My inside fell and I found it hard to breathe. There was a
rustle in the room: the class were shifting in their seats to take
a look at me. I got up. I could hardly read the print in front of
me because my hand was shaking.

With an effort I pulled myself together and taking a deep
breath I started translating. My voice was as firm as I could
make it, but as my words dropped into the silence I had no idea
what impression they were making. I felt at any moment a storm
might break...

It did.

After a verse or two I arrived at the word ἀναστροφήν which
I translated 'conversion'.

'Conversion—' I said.

'What!' It was as if someone had fired a shot from the other
end of the room.

I looked up.

'Go back to the word ἀναστροφήν,' rapped out Jimmy.

'ἀναστροφήν', I repeated, looking down at the book again, 'conversion.'

'Conversion, eh?' echoed Jimmy. 'Have you prepared this
lesson?'

'Yes, sir.'

'Oh, sir! Indeed, sir!' observed the Headmaster, in ironic
imitation of my voice. He then set about fumbling for his pince-

nez glasses. 'Let me get out my eagle eye,' he added, glancing round with what I took to be a good-humoured twinkle. The class tittered, and thinking that my mistake (whatever it might be) was going to be treated leniently, even perhaps with jocosity, I also smiled. It was a weak, nervous smile, with no heartiness behind it, but it was enough of a smile to upset Jimmy.

The noise of his shouting suddenly filled the room.

'Smiling, sir! You dare to treat this as a smiling matter! Stand up on the form, you little beast! D'you hear me, stand up on the form!'

When Jimmy was angry he always shouted and called you names, like 'dirty beast', 'dingy toad', and so on. It was a habit of his.

Now I was frightened. I climbed up on the form, while Jimmy glared at me through his glasses. The room was silent.

'Now, sir,' he rapped out fiercely. 'You tell me you prepared this lesson.'

I stared back at him, and my muttered 'yes' evidently did not reach his ears.

'Answer me!' he shouted.

'Yes, sir.'

'And when you came to the word "ἀναστροφήν"—what did you do?'

What had I done? I could remember nothing.

'Well, sir, I am waiting,' exclaimed Jimmy.

'I don't remember, sir,' I said.

'What! You don't remember!'

'No, sir.'

'Did you look the word up in the lexicon?' he demanded.

I tried to think what I had done. My gaze strayed over to Jeffries and Pethick with whom I had prepared the lesson. But their eyes were on their books in front of them. What *had* we done?

'I don't remember, sir,' I repeated lamely.

'And yet you say you prepared the lesson, you slovenly lout! You stand there and have the impudence to tell me you prepared the lesson! You did nothing of the kind! You thought you wouldn't be called upon, eh, was that it? You thought you wouldn't be called upon!'

Up to now Jimmy's tone had been *crescendo*. Suddenly his voice altered to a sinister bass.

'Shall I tell you what you did?' he demanded ominously. 'Heark'ee to this—' (Jimmy now and then indulged in archaisms) ' "For ye have heard of my conversation in time past in the Jews' religion." Do you recognise that, sir, eh? Do you recognise that?'

'Yes, sir,' I said.

'So! Your idea of preparing this lesson was to use the Bible as a crib!'

Put like that the case against me assumed vaster and weightier proportions. What before was a crime was now a sin.

'Was that it, eh?' went on Jimmy, adopting the *crescendo* tone again. 'You debased the Holy Scriptures by using them as a crib, you filthy rat! And even so you couldn't take the trouble to use the crib correctly!'

I think at this point he must have noticed the tears on my cheeks. For he suddenly gave over shouting. 'A discreditable performance,' he muttered, taking off his glasses. 'A disgusting performance. You will spend this afternoon copying out the notes of the whole chapter and bring them to me by four o'clock...'

Glancing at Professor Ramsay's notes on other chapters I couldn't help feeling that he had spread himself unduly on Chapter I. However, I didn't have to play football—which was something.

VI

In time I grew to understand Jimmy and to like him. He was not so fine a scholar as H. H. House, the sixth-form master who held open wide the doors of learning for us. But there was about Jimmy a boyishness that made a strong appeal to young people. He was 'a sport', with an eye for the humorous side of any situation. A new boy running along the corridor (and so breaking one of the school rules) turned a corner and bumped heavily into the Headmaster. Jimmy fumed.

'What's your scrubby name?' he demanded.

'James, sir,' replied the boy promptly. Whereupon the elder James's wrath evaporated.

'Hmph!' he grunted. 'It's not such a scrubby name after all. Get along with you.'

Incidents like that—and they could be multiplied—contributed much to Jimmy's popularity.

Even his fierceness in form—as I discovered later when I was in the Sixth and attended his classes every day—established a relationship between him and his pupils which was not empty of affection. Failure to prepare your lesson meant trouble. But the successful preparation of it, the earning of, say, four marks out of the almost unattainable five, elicited a nod which somehow or other made up for all the sweat you had been through. Fear of the consequences was gradually overlaid by pride in one's work as the chief incentive to do one's best and 'to get the thing right'. But the line between fear and pride was finely drawn.

Jimmy's fierceness was also mitigated by an occasional geniality which was irresistible. Now and then he would break off the lesson and tell us some story of his own early days as a schoolboy, or as an assistant-master at Eton. The story was nearly always against himself. At such moments you were sensible of privilege. You were one of an exclusive set. To recount afterwards details of Jimmy's early life, as told to you by the great man himself, was to boast of an intimacy which very few boys in the school could ever share.

Towards the end of his reign at Malvern—he left in 1914—his temper mellowed. Perhaps he sensed the changing spirit of the times. More probably his indulgence was due to age. But he never lost his vigour or his grip. On the last three Sundays of his last term he preached three sermons on the Pauline text: 'Stand fast in the faith: quit you like men: be strong.' The text and the sermons were characteristic of the preacher. Weakness, indecision, slothfulness were outside his make-up, and he did not encourage these qualities in others.

VII

Two more memories of Malvern. The first: speech-week in the summer of 1914, a mixture of solemnity and junketing. A chapel service of commemoration: prize-giving and speech-making, what time I read my English poem on Isaiah, and the local M.P. told us that the future lay in our hands. A special parade of the school O.T.C., inspected by a real General : and throughout the week meals at hotels with one's own or other people's parents.

The culmination of the festival was the annual cricket match against the Old Boys, as important in its way as the commemoration service. You didn't have to crack jokes about this cricket match. Nothing short of double pneumonia would have excused you from attending it.

The crowd that gathered there was a microcosm of our world. Well-dressed, good-humoured, and naturally self-assured, they represented for us boys the kind of society into which we ourselves were soon to pass. To have asked questions about that society would have been to show oneself a fool. One might as well have asked questions about the Bank of England or the ground beneath one's feet. Doubt and uncertainty about the future there was none. We knew, each of us, how our paths were set, what careers we were to follow, or at all events what careers were open to us. We knew—though we never thought about it—that we belonged to a respected class whose members it was customary for waiters, railway porters and such like to address as 'sir' : and we knew that whatever happened we must always be true to the code. The nature of this code had been defined for us by Jimmy in three words—'Christian English Gentlemen' : and by Roley Lyon, with greater economy, in two —'Old Malvernian'. These things we knew. Once they had been grasped, all extra knowledge could be looked upon as trimmings.

The world then was stable and for us at the time the speech-week crowd, watching the Old Boys' match, marked no more than one episode in the continuity of things, one of a succession of events that stretched back long before our time and would extend into the future for as far as any of us cared to look ahead.

That this gathering was in fact to mark the end of a chapter, the close of what is sometimes conceived of as a golden age, was a thought that could not have occurred to any of us.

A few weeks later I was in the school O.T.C. camp near Aldershot. In spite of my three stripes, conferred upon me because I was a school prefect and could not very well have remained a private, my authority was nominal. I had not the instinct of command, and no one, not even the latest-joined recruit, took the slightest notice of anything I said. A further embarrassment was that I suffered from spots on my neck and back, and throughout the battalion I was known as 'Spotty'. Boys on parade addressed me as 'Spotty', saying, 'Yes, Spotty', instead of 'Yes, Sergeant'.

The camp was supposed to last for a fortnight and at the end of the first three days I wondered how I was going to endure it. Mercifully there was news in the papers that was causing some excitement. A murder, it seemed, had been committed a month or so beforehand at a place called Sarajevo. War, we were told, might break out at any moment between England and Germany. Everybody wondered what was going to happen. To me the news was doubly welcome : it directed attention away from my spots : and it meant that if war *were* to break out, the camp would be closed and we should be sent home. Naturally I prayed that war would be declared. When on the fifth day of camp my prayer was granted, no one thanked God more wholeheartedly than I did.

We were sent home in our uniforms. As I emerged from Baker Street Station on my way home to Hampstead a little knot of people raised a cheer for me because they thought I was a soldier off to the war. Apart from the affair of the collar at Stallard's, it was my first taste of public admiration—and it was based on a misunderstanding.

VIII

One afternoon at the beginning of September Maurice Haighwood, a boy who lived near us at Hampstead and had also been at Malvern though not in my House, burst into our drawing-room and announced that he had joined the Inns of Court O.T.C. He was full of enthusiasm and begged me to join too. Up to that moment I had been perplexed about the war. It had not occurred to me that my life would be affected by it. Wars were the affairs of armies and navies and did not touch civilians. Anyway I was not yet eighteen and had another year to go at Malvern. Also I was reading for a scholarship at Cambridge. So all things considered I did not see that the war, which everybody said would be over by Christmas, was going to affect me at all.

Then Maurice appeared.

His enthusiasm woke me up. He was the answer to everything —a marvellous chance of ending my career at Malvern and a glorious opportunity to serve the country! My horizon suddenly widened. Up to now my life had been conceived in terms of private activity; of serving one's own career. The idea of being identified with some great cause and of throwing oneself heart and soul into its service had seemed utterly remote. It was the sort of thing one might have read about in books: great soldiers, for example, winning historic battles and being met by the King at the station on their return (but then I was not going to be a soldier); or great explorers leading expeditions to the North Pole (but then I was not going to be an explorer); or famous Empire-builders founding new countries (but then I was not going to be an Empire-builder: I had, I was told, my living to earn). These were dreams, realisable by other people. They related to nothing that I was ever likely to encounter.

And now, by some extraordinary turn of events, all that was changed.

It is difficult at this distance of time to be sure about motives. I suspect that what really moved me was less a feeling of patriotism than a desire to stand right with my fellows. To have been a conscientious objector at Malvern--even if I had wanted to be one—would have been unthinkable.

I got wild with excitement. I thanked God for Maurice. I thanked God for the Inns of Court O.T.C. I thanked God for everything that had happened. All that remained was to get the necessary permission.

That evening I saw my father. His presence sobered me a little. But I was confident.

'I want to join the Inns of Court O.T.C.' I said. As soon as I had spoken I felt a sense of misgiving. A few hours before I myself would have been staggered at the thought. Now that the idea had seized me nothing seemed more natural than that I should join the Army.

Father's first look of astonishment gave way to a smile.

'What's put that idea into your head?'' he asked.

'Maurice Haighwood's joined,' I replied. 'And I want to join too. I *must* join.'

'Maurice Haighwood? He's older than you are.'

'Only a year older.'

'Well, a year's a year,' observed my father. 'Besides, he's left Malvern, hasn't he?'

'Well, I've been there four years,' I said. 'It's quite long enough.'

'What about your scholarship?'

'I can't help that—'

My father chuckled. It was plain that he had no intention of letting me go.

'Boys of seventeen—' he said.

'Eighteen,' I interrupted. I was just eighteen that August.

'Well, boys of eighteen, then,' he resumed, 'aren't wanted in the Army. The best way you can serve the country is by going on with your schooling, so that you'll be ready after the war's over to . . .'

'To what?' I growled.

'To go on with your career.'

Just so! But what did my career matter compared with England's need of me! The thing, I felt, was beyond argument. So indeed did my father: only his conclusion was the opposite to mine. I pleaded with him, and used every reason I could think of to prove what to me was an axiom. But he refused to budge. All he promised was that when I had finished my time at Malvern—that is, at the end of another twelve months—'he would see'.

My state was one between anger and misery. But I did not have the courage to enlist without permission.

IX

In December I went up for my scholarship exam at Cambridge. There were very few undergraduates about and the University population consisted mainly of elderly or very aged dons and unfit students. The sight of them and of the deserted colleges added to the sense of futility from which I was suffering. More of my friends had joined up since August. Howard Hill had gone. So had Jeffries. Almost every day I was hearing of other boys of my own age who had received or been promised commissions. And here was I—still messing about at the same old game, still having to plough my way through Greek and Latin unseens and turn English verse into elegiacs and iambics.

I went about in a distracted state, so much so that on one occasion I got into the wrong group and did the wrong exam. On discovering my mistake I went to the Senior Tutor of my college, who put me on my honour not to look at the paper which my group had done that morning and arranged for me to sit in his spare room the same evening and take the exam which I had missed. The arrangement was, I was told, without precedent.

When a few weeks later my name appeared among the successful competitors, I was not much elated. I would rather have been listed in the *London Gazette* as a Second Lieutenant. As it was, I begged my father to let me off my last two terms at Malvern, seeing that I had now taken my scholarship and would only be wasting my time by staying on.

But nothing I could say would move him.

My last half-year at Malvern was a blank period. Like all blank periods it seemed interminable. Being by now a school prefect I was subjected only to very occasional ragging—as when for example I was put in charge of a school run. These runs were supervised by two school prefects, one who led the pack, the other who brought up the rear and carried a hunting crop. The pace at which I could run unfitted me to be the leader of the pack : it was even inadequate for bringing up the rear. The consequence was that I was always too far behind to make any use of my hunting-crop, even if I had wanted to. And of course I came in for all the usual jibes.

However, on the whole, I was allowed to live an unmolested life. But I took no interest in it. The few friends I had made had already left to join up. All I lived for was to do the same.

PART TWO

'THE GREAT ADVENTURE'

I

MY FATHER INSISTED that I should wait until my nineteenth birthday before joining the Army, which meant that three weeks had to be disposed of after I left Malvern. This period I spent with my mother and father at Weston-super-Mare. So that the time might not be wholly wasted, I spent it growing a moustache.

Then on the 21st of August, 1915, I joined the Inns of Court O.T.C. and took the oath of allegiance in the Old Hall of Lincoln's Inn.

By contrast with the years that had gone before, the month I spent drilling in Lincoln's Inn Fields was very heaven. The school O.T.C. had taught me the details of the drill and I had no fear of making a fool of myself over that. But the new and surprising thing for me was that even if I had made a fool of myself no one would have ragged me, or even laughed at me. The crowd I was with were not on the look-out for duffers. The thing that mattered was that you should learn the job and learn it properly. If you were slow at it or nervous or even inefficient, so far from laughing at you the other fellows were glad to help you out.

For me the change was welcome. I had no longer to worry about my defects or my personal peculiarities. I felt that I was living among friends.

At the end of a month the company was moved to the training camp at Berkhamsted, and the loss of the home life which I had enjoyed in London was made up by the kindness of the family on whom I was billeted. Through my father's influence the local bank manager and his wife opened their home to me. The Webbs were simple people. Mr. Webb was devoted to his job and to the welfare of the neighbourhood in which he lived. He had more than once been offered promotion which would have meant moving to another part of England : but he had always refused, preferring to remain in Berkhamsted. His wife divided her time between looking after her family (there was one son and one daughter) and caring for the poor of the district, where her work was never ostentatious. For that reason she was one of the best loved women in the town.

Mr. Webb's hobby was carpentry. At the back of the house there was a barn which he had fitted up as a work-shop. I used to spend a good deal of my spare time there with him, partly because I enjoyed working in wood, but mainly because I enjoyed Mr. Webb's company. His zest in the work was genuine. So was the pleasure he took in explaining its mysteries. I was fascinated by his intense concentration. Everything he valued in life might have been depending on the way a particular piece of wood was planed or spoke-shaved. From the hour of the next meal to the war itself nothing seemed of any importance beside the job which Mr. Webb happened to be doing at the moment.

Whenever I think of the Webbs I think of their drawing-room. It was a room that summed them up. With its glass-doored china-cupboards, its old-fashioned ornaments, its rarely-used grand piano, laden with silver-framed photographs, its slightly musty smell (for the room was used only for Sunday afternoon tea) and its general air of dusty tranquillity, this drawing-room represented all that one felt the Webbs stood for in a changing world. For me at the time that room became identified with the past, with Victorian tradition, with the stability of things which was being threatened. There must have been many rooms like it all over England : but I never came across one that gave off quite the same Sunday-evening-church-bells-Abide-With-Me atmosphere. Our own drawing-room at home came somewhere near it, but it was never such a quiet room as the Webbs' and it did not hold so many ancient ornaments and knick-knacks.

II

'No. 5026, Private Thomas, sir !'

The sergeant-major saluted and withdrew, leaving me alone with the Colonel, a white-haired, venerable-looking gentleman with two rows of ribbons on his tunic.

'Well, Thomas,' he began, 'I see you've been gazetted now to the...let me see...yes, to the Royal West Kents. A fine regiment. A very fine regiment. Well, I hope you've benefited from your time here and learnt something of what's expected from an officer. Taking His Majesty's Commission is a responsibility which...'

I listened as he talked but I do not think I took in what he said. All I was conscious of was that the long-awaited hour had come when I would be able to wear an officer's uniform. Henceforth I would be in command of a platoon and entitled to a salute from everyone from the Battalion Sergeant-major downwards! But the knowledge was accompanied by misgivings. Would I be able to do the job? Would I succeed in commanding the respect of my men? Would they obey me? Above all, would I have the courage to lead them as they should be led? Or would I only succeed in making a fool of myself? In the O.T.C. I had been obscured in the ranks: and even when I had been hauled out and made to take charge of a platoon or of a company everyone had known that the thing was a practice. We had all been friends together. But now the real test was coming. Would I be up to it?

'....and I'm sure that you'll uphold the traditions not only of your own regiment but also of "The Devil's Own".'

I found myself shaking hands with the Colonel and being wished good luck.

III

I got out of the train at Tonbridge feeling very 'new', self-conscious and lonely. I had no friends or even acquaintances in the Territorial battalion to which I had been posted, though the Colonel, I understood, was a friend of my father's.

I drove to the address I had been given, a largish villa in a very respectable row. The small approach was flanked by laurels and the house looked as if it might have been the home of a comfortable solicitor.

The front door was open and the cabman deposited my luggage in the hall. It was about three o'clock in the afternoon and the place seemed deserted. I stood for a moment, wondering

2—ALA

where I ought to go. There were various doors leading off the
hall, some open, some closed. I peeped through one that opened
into an empty dining-room. Then I tip-toed across the hall and
looked in at another open door. This, as it turned out, was the
Orderly Room, where an officer was sitting at a table, writing.

I went in, coughing apologetically. The officer looked up.

'Good afternoon sir,' I said.

I saw from the two stars on his sleeve that he was not the
Colonel.

'Hullo,' he nodded in a friendly way. 'You just turned up?'

'Yes, I've been posted to this battalion.'

He nodded and invited me to 'take a pew'. He didn't, he said,
quite know where I was to sleep but when the Colonel came back
he would fix things. 'Meanwhile,' he added, leading the way into
the mess, 'you'd better have a drink.'

My first thought was of tea.

'That's very kind of you,' I said. 'I wouldn't mind some—'
I was going to say 'I wouldn't mind some tea.' But at the appearance of a rather fierce-looking orderly with a black moustache
waxed at the tips, my voice faded out.

'Bring a couple of large whiskies, Shoesmith,' ordered my host.

I had not been brought up a teetotaller, though my father was
the most abstemious of men. When he came home tired after a
heavy day's work or when he had been out in the wet he might
take a very weak whisky and soda. Otherwise he drank water
with his meals, with possibly a glass of ale at lunch on Sundays. I
never at any time heard of him drinking between meals. I myself
had never drunk anything stronger than ale. The idea of drinking
whisky at four o'clock in the afternoon was new and rather
shocking.

'Oh, please,' I exclaimed, 'I don't think I'll have whisky—
though it's very kind of you.'

The officer nodded.

'Prefer a gin-and-tonic?' he enquired.

I became confused. What I would have liked was tea : but tea
seemed too remote to mention.

'I think, if you don't mind,' I said, 'I'll have ginger beer.'

'Gin and ginger?' he queried as though he had misheard.

'No, just plain ginger beer.'

There was a slightly puzzled look on his face as he gave the order. I felt I had sunk to zero in his estimation.

'You just got your commission?' he enquired, with a suppressed yawn.

'Yes—a week ago.'

He nodded. 'Feels a bit strange to begin with, I expect.'

'Yes, a bit,' I agreed. I wondered how long he had held a commission, but I didn't dare to ask.

'You'll soon get into it,' he remarked absently. 'I'm the Assistant-Adjutant.'

When the drinks came mine was handed to me first. As he took his I noticed that he signed a chit.

'It's very good of you . . .' I murmured.

He smiled, said 'Cheerio' and drank his whisky with astonishing speed.

Just as I had taken a sip of my ginger beer he got up and said that he must go and write some letters.

'I expect the others'll be in before long,' he added, and left me to myself.

I felt that I had not made much of an impression.

IV

That evening I was introduced to the Colonel. I had expected the C.O. to be a tall, lean, hard-bitten man, with at least two rows of medals—terribly efficient and exacting. I think I must have got that impression from seeing a Colonel of the Coldstream Guards who had once inspected us in the school O.T.C.—a devil of a fellow he had seemed and no doubt was. The Colonel who commanded my present battalion was not like that at all. He was short and plump and gave the impression of soft living. He reminded me at once of Roley, though Roley's bearing had been more military. The C.O. did not in fact look like a soldier at all. He looked like a city man and his manners had the silkiness of a financier's.

He greeted me with civility and a flabby handshake. He hoped that I would be happy with the battalion and added that the adjutant would tell me which company I was to join.

I thanked him and screwed up enough courage to say that my father wished to be remembered to him.

The C.O. looked puzzled. Then he remembered.

'Ah, yes, of course—your father. An old friend of mine. I hope he's well.'

'Very well, thank you, sir.'

'That's good. You must remember me to him when you write.'

'I will, sir.'

'Do. And . . . and I hope that you're going to enjoy your time with us.'

I had the impression of distant courtesy. There was no coldness: nor was there warmth. Nothing repellent: nothing attractive. But somehow my meeting with him emphasised my sense of loneliness.

That night I asked one of the officers whose bedroom I shared what sort of chap the C.O. was.

'D'you play bridge?' he asked. I said that I did not.

'In that case, you won't see much of the C.O.'

Nor did I. For at the end of my first week at Tonbridge I was sent away on a musketry course to Hythe. The course lasted a month which was extended in my case for another fortnight so that I could take a course of range-finding. By that time a new battalion had been formed and I was posted to it. I never in fact returned to Tonbridge at all.

V

The new battalion to which I was posted was stationed at Cambridge, the officers being quartered in Magdalene College, and the men in the boat-houses.

Whether it was that I had been in Cambridge before and felt attached to the place, or that having held my commission now for over two months I was beginning to feel my feet, or that on my arrival I was given sole charge of a platoon—whatever the reason, at Cambridge I felt for the first time that I was beginning to lead a satisfying life. I was one of a company, each of whom had a definite job and all of whom were engaged on a common task. We were in training. Our object was to make ourselves as fit and efficient as possible. It never occurred to anyone to doubt our cause or to think that peace could come except through victory. For me it was enough that I was in the Army and that we might all of us soon go out to France.

In this I was wrong. Our battalion, it seemed, was not to go out as a unit, but was a reserve for feeding other battalions in the regiment. As these other battalions were stationed in different parts of the world—France, Egypt, Palestine, India—it was not at all certain where you would be sent. All I could do was to put my name down on the waiting-list for France and trust to luck. More disheartening still was the knowledge that when the time came for us to go, we should all be separated. Here we were a community, working together, getting to know each other and getting to know our men. Day in, day out, we spent most of our time in their company, drilling them, lecturing them, taking them for route marches, sharing experiences with them, talking to them off parade and in their billets, learning the strength and weakness of each one of them, finding out which of them could be trusted with responsibility, which were keen, which were lazy, which groused, which bore life cheerfully, which could be relied on in a tight corner and which would never make soldiers however long you trained them. All this knowledge we were acquiring: and the more we acquired of it the more efficient as a battalion we became. Yet we knew that when the time came we should all be scattered, probably in different continents. That meant that we should have to start all over again as strangers to the men we should command.

The system was probably inevitable: but it gave us the feeling that much of our work was wasted and that personal loyalties—of the men to their officers and of the junior officers to their seniors—would never be tested.

Seven months I spent with this battalion, first at Cambridge and later at Crowborough, and as the days passed I grew more impatient. From time to time I heard of friends who had been killed, wounded, taken prisoner or reported missing. It was during this summer that Charles Jeffries had a narrow escape on the

Somme. A bullet injured his vocal chords. Now he was back in England and would soon be 'invalided out'. Howard Hill had already been six months in France and was shortly coming home on leave. Maurice Haighwood wrote to say that he had just been having 'a marvellous time on Paris leave'—and when was I coming out?...

The Colonel understood my impatience. It was shared by all the young officers in the battalion. But he was as powerless as any of us to hasten the day of our going. If the decision had rested with him he would have taken the whole battalion overseas himself, and been glad to do so. As it was, his active service days were over. A regular, wearing the South African ribbon, he had been recalled from the retired list and given charge of a Reserve battalion. A tall, spare man, he was delicate in health and (so we were told) subject to epileptic fits. Certainly his temper was uneven. But while we feared him we also respected him. For we recognised in him that quality of soldierliness which comes only with long service. Having him as our Colonel we felt that we were more than amateurs. (Years later, long after the war, I was surprised when he asked me if I knew of a job that would suit him. Times were hard and he was finding it difficult to live on his pension. Unfortunately I knew of nothing, as the kind of work I was doing was not in his line. A year later, I met him again at a battalion dinner at the Trocadero. He seemed in better spirits this time and confided to me that he had found a job. When I asked him what it was, he replied: 'You'll never guess. I've gone on the stage.' That evening, at about twenty past eight, just after the fish had been served, he got up from the table and begged the company to excuse him, as he had, as he put it, to go on parade. All he did was walk up the road to the Shaftesbury Theatre, remove the medals from his evening dress and walk straight on to the stage—in the rôle of a butler.)

The summer dragged on—a summer for me of peace-time soldiering, impatience and a dread lest I should be sent to India (as I nearly was) instead of to France. Every day we followed the news, read of victories and defeats, of battles with thousands of casualties, of enemy ships captured, of our own ships sunk by

U-boats. In June a concert was interrupted for the news of Kitchener's death to be announced.

At intervals drafts of men, in charge of an officer, were sent off, sometimes to France, more often to India or to the Near East. For days beforehand the draft would be paraded, fitted out, inspected, lectured and generally brought up to scratch. On the day of their departure they would be addressed by the Colonel and then played out of the camp by the battalion band to the tune of 'A Hundred Pipers', which was our Regimental March. We envied the drafts for France and wondered when our turn was coming.

Not that we spent the whole summer talking and thinking of nothing but being sent abroad. But in all our thoughts there was an undercurrent of impatience. It bubbled to the surface mostly when we were away from camp. On leave or when we were visiting private houses in the neighbourhood people would ask us where we had been serving, how long we had been out, whether we had been wounded, and so on. And we would reply, rather shame-facedly, that so far we had not been out of England. But apart from what other people might think, we did feel in our hearts that we wanted to share the danger—and the glory. We felt above all that we too 'wanted to be there'.

The summer passed into autumn. Then on October the first, word came that in a week's time I was to 'proceed overseas'.

'Where?' I asked, in a sweat of anxiety. 'Where am I to go?'

The adjutant smiled, knowing what was in my mind.

'You're going to France,' he said.

VI

There were seven of us in that draft—seven subalterns, one of whom, H. J. Dunn, was a special friend of mine. Dunn had been an assistant librarian in the Bodleian. He was a quiet, gentle creature, regarded by those who didn't know him as 'superior'. The truth was that his manner was protective. After the seclusion of the University it wasn't easy for him to adjust himself to the rough-and-tumble and vulgarity of Army life. He found things and people 'distressing': So-and-so was 'a most distressing per-

son' : so were Captain X's lectures or Major Y's jokes or the way
that Sergeant Z roared at his squad on parade—all were 'distressing'. In order to protect himself against these constant onslaughts
on his sensitiveness, he had grown an outer crust which was generally known as 'Dunn's damned superior manner'.

The quality in him which attracted me most was his mildly
ironical outlook, the way he had of suggesting, more by his
manner than by words, that nothing in life need be taken too
seriously—not even death. In the daily routine of camp life he
had an enviable capacity for allowing problems to solve themselves. Laziness? Certainly Dunn was not energetic. Yet there was
never anything to find fault with in the way he managed his
platoon and particularly in the way he looked after the welfare
of his men. He never obtruded. He never bustled round. Except
when he was giving words of command, he never raised his voice
above a tone that was just audible. But one word from him,
whether it was in the mess or among his men, was more effective
than a dozen words from anybody else.

I was naturally pleased that he was coming out to France
with me. I hoped—and I think he hoped too—that we would be
posted to the same battalion. Between ourselves we referred to
our going as 'The Great Adventure'. But the twinkle in his eye
relieved the phrase of all pomposity. An adventure, certainly :
but also a bit of a jest.

Three of the others in our draft I also knew well. The gayest
and most attractive of them was H. S. Mitchell, affectionately
known as 'Young Mitch', because there was another and older
Mitchell in the battalion. 'Young Mitch' was a high-spirited boy,
of no particular gifts, but desperately keen to take his share of
duty : keen to be where the danger was greatest : keen, if need
be, to die leading his men in battle. (One knew somehow that
'Young Mitch' would be taken. Less than a year later he died
in the way he would have wished.)

Martin Hay was a quiet fellow, but without any of the charm,
personality or distinction of Dunn, or the high spirits or keenness
of 'Young Mitch'. He was indeed an exception to most of us,
because he had no real desire to go to France at all. In civil life
he was a solicitor and his home was in Sydenham. This latter

fact was known to everyone, because Hay never tired of mentioning it. 'I'm a home bird, you know,' he would say to anyone who would listen. 'I live in Sydenham: lived there all my life, you know. Wish I was there now.' A paraphrase of Sophocles' famous lines might well have been applied to Hay: 'The best thing of all is never to have left Sydenham: the next best thing having left Sydenham, is to return there as quickly as possible.' He was a conscientious officer, but his chief concern was to see that his men were comfortable rather than efficient. 'Home comfort' were words which, I fancy, meant a lot to Hay.

The third man, Clarence Budd, was a dour, sardonic type. His black hair, yellowish complexion and general immobility of features gave an impression of oriental inscrutability. He had few friends—which was not surprising, seeing that he showed no interest in other people. In fact I do not think I ever met anyone so indifferent to his fellows, to his surroundings or to his probable fate as Clarence Budd. To me, who had shared a bedroom with him in the huts at Crowborough, he was invariably civil and well-disposed. But we were not close friends. The remaining two men I knew only as casual acquaintances.

As there were no men in our draft, we were not 'played' out of camp. We left unobtrusively in three taxis, drove nine miles to Tunbridge Wells, and joined the Folkestone train. The country looked lovely. The leaves were on the turn and the landscape was yielding to autumn's melancholy.

In the train Martin Hay leant over to me and said: 'You know, I've never been out of England before. Have you?' I replied that I had, several times. 'I haven't,' repeated Hay, with a shake of his head. 'And I never thought that when I did, it'd be to go and fight. Why,' he added, in a burst of resentment, 'I may never see the place again!' He looked at me, demanding reassurance. But before I could answer, he went on: 'But *you* don't mind, do you? You don't mind leaving England.'

'I don't want to get killed, if that's what you mean,' I said feebly. 'I want to come back.'

Hay sighed and, shifting his gaze out of the window, relapsed into silence.

'Live from day to day—and don't think,' Dunn had once

advised me. That wasn't difficult at twenty. Still, Hay was right.
We—he, I, any of us—*might* never see the place again. This
might be our last journey. And that was the truth of it, though
judging from our spirits no one would have thought it.

'Would you go back now?' I said to Hay, 'if you had the
chance? Supposing when we get to Folkestone there was an order
saying that there was a mistake about your coming and that
you'd got to go back to Crowborough, would you be glad?'

'Yes,' he said promptly. 'I would. I'd go back like a shot.
Wouldn't you?'

I chuckled. I think I was surprised at his frankness. It was a
challenge to me to say what I thought.

'I think,' I replied, 'that I'd be disappointed.'

'I wouldn't,' said Hay. 'I hate leaving home. And I hate this
bloody war. I'm not a soldier, Thomas. I never was.'

Nor was I, I felt. As for hating the war, I didn't see the point
of that either. We were in the war and the only thing to do was
to win it! I had heard of people—'conchies' they were called
—who hated war on principle and refused to join up. But one
didn't take them seriously. Names like Ramsay Macdonald or
Philip Snowden were not to us then the names of progressive
men, but of traitors or at best misguided fools. 'Conchies' to us
were like lepers: one avoided them. That was the state of mind
we were in. So when Hay talked of hating war I looked at him
—though I knew of course that he wasn't one of *them*.

'But surely—' I began, not quite knowing what I was going to
say.

'I don't,' Hay interrupted me, 'see what there'd be to be
disappointed about.'

'Don't you?' I said, losing patience a little.

At that moment somebody suggested drinks. I thought 'To
hell with Hay! What do I care what he thinks. I prefer Dunn's
view—a Great Adventure on the borderline of a Great Joke.'

VII

The sight of the destroyers which convoyed us across the
Channel was exhilarating. They made us feel we were people

who mattered. They also reminded us of Britain's command of the seas: and that pleased us, giving us a sense of our superiority. 'Fancy anyone imagining,' somebody said, 'that the Germans stand an earthly!' Though I met people who felt they would never come back, I never met anyone who doubted that the Allies would win.

At Boulogne we fetched up at the Hotel du Louvre, opposite the station, where we spent the night. I had been to Boulogne before. Also I could speak a little French. But the real reason why I talked to the liftman who saw me to my room was that on landing in France I wanted, as it were, to cement our common cause. I wanted to assure him that I, an Englishman, was glad to salute him, a Frenchman: and that I felt proud to be standing by his side in our common task—or words to that effect.

It was a generous, if sentimental, impulse. Whether a liftman at a third-rate provincial hotel was the best person to choose as the recipient of this tribute may be doubted. The manager of the hotel, or even the Maire might have seemed a more suitable choice. But neither the Maire nor the manager was present: and the liftman was. That at least was a point in his favour. The man, however, proved extremely unresponsive. At first he seemed to have no idea what I was talking about. Then as my little speech developed (this all took place inside my bedroom) a look of devastating enlightenment came into his face. He saw that I was an escaped lunatic or a religious fanatic. After that he frowned, for he had perceived that I was not mad, but serious, and that I was talking about the war and about the English and the French. He thereupon interrupted my speech in order to express his deep disgust not merely with the war, but also with the conditions of life which it imposed, particularly upon him: with the hours he worked, with the wages he drew, with the kind of food he had to put up with, with the high cost of living, and with the absence of anything like an adequate tipping system. The English, on the other hand, always appeared to have plenty of money, judging from the extravagant use they made of it in every possible way except in the handing out of tips. As for the war, the sooner it was over the better. The impression left on me was that one

of the reasons for welcoming its end would be the consequent
return of the English to their island.

I confess I was disillusioned by this man. I felt that he could
not be representative of the spirit of France about which I had
read so much in the papers. The way he kept shrugging his
shoulders, raising his eyebrows and expressing contempt by making a noise between a whistle and a hiss was not in line with that
singleness of purpose which I understood was the essence of the
French attitude, or indeed with the cordiality with which the
people of France were supposed to welcome their allies. This
man, I told myself, was a disgruntled fellow. I wished I had left
my little speech unspoken.

I was often to visit that hotel in my journeys to and fro on
leave : but I never saw the liftman again. Perhaps he had been
given a week's notice on the day I met him and was feeling his
position. Perhaps he was a born pessimist and ended by com-
mitting suicide. But whatever became of him, the dark possibility
that he was reflecting the opinion of his fellow-countrymen did
not occur to me.

Next day we left by train for the base camp at Etaples and by
what seemed an unnecessary stroke of inconvenience we reached
there between eleven and twelve o'clock at night.

A base camp is an unsatisfactory place to stay in at any time
(except for those who run it) and its attractions, if any, are certainly lost on a newcomer who turns up round about midnight,
particularly if it happens to be raining hard, as it was when we
arrived. Every place of refreshment had been closed and there
was nothing for us to do but to grope our way to the tents that
had been allotted to us and lie down in our clothes.

The trouble about Etaples was the feeling of loose-endishness
it gave you. There you were, doing parades which couldn't interest you because you knew that you were only doing them to
fill in time. For the rest you wandered about, knowing that at
any hour of the day or night you might be ordered away. More
than ever you felt at the mercy of a huge, impersonal machine
which might pick you up at any moment or might forget all
about you and leave you lying about for weeks, sometimes
months. There was nothing you could do either to hasten or to

delay things. The only thing left was to pray for your name to be called. Meanwhile, loose-endishness easily merged into loneliness. You met a man you liked : the next day he would be gone : whereas the fellow whose company you had decided to avoid seemed always in the path.

On this occasion I was lucky : for the seven of us were still together, and at first there was plenty to occupy our time. Deficiencies in our kit had to be made good : the gas hut had to be visited to make sure that our flannel gas masks were in working order : lectures had to be attended for officers who had come out for the first time. And by way of relaxation there was Paris Plage. But forty-eight hours of the Base Camp were enough for most of us and when on the third day Young Mitch and another were ordered off, we envied them. 'Good luck!' we shouted as their train moved out and returning disconsolately to the camp we waited impatiently for our turn to come.

At the end of a week we were still waiting. Then on the eighth day, just as we were thinking of sending an ultimatum to the Adjutant, orders came for one more of us to go—myself. Young Mitch and the other had been posted to the seventh battalion and I had been hoping that Dunn and I might go there too. But my chit said I was to join the sixth battalion. Dunn had received no chit at all.

'You're going to join the sixth, eh?' grinned the Adjutant, as I took my leave of him.

'What's the joke?' I asked.

'The Colonel of the sixth's a fine chap,' murmured the Adjutant. 'He's known as "The Fire-Eater!" Good luck!'

It was Martin Hay who said, when I told him of it, that he didn't much like the sound of the Adjutant's remark. I laughed —partly to keep my spirits up, but also at the expression on Martin Hay's face as he mouthed the word 'fire-eater'.

'You laugh!' he observed.

'Only thing to do,' I said. 'P'raps you'll be posted to the sixth as well. I hope so.'

Hay was torn between appreciation of the compliment and hatred of fire-eaters.

'I don't know about that,' he muttered mournfully.

That evening Dunn saw me off at the railway siding. We
both wished that we had been going on The Great Adventure
together. But we had not lost all hope that even yet he might be
posted to the sixth.

'If you do come,' I said, 'I'll jolly well see that we're in the
same company! It would be fun!'

Dunn smiled. I think he was amused at my enthusiasm.

'Let's hope it comes true,' he said quietly.

'Rather!'

I was leaning out of the carriage window now and Dunn was
standing by the side of the track, far below me. As he looked
up and down the train he was gently tapping his leg with his
cane.

'If you don't come to the sixth,' I said, 'let me know where
you *do* land up.'

He promised this. Then a wailing note sounded from the
stationmaster's horn and we began to move.

'Good luck!' said Dunn. 'Look after yourself!'

'Same to you,' I said. 'See you soon!'

He gave a little waggle with his cane, and then turned away
towards the steep path that led up the side of the embankment
to the camp. He had just reached the foot of the path when I
lost sight of him—for good.

VIII

For one night and one day I and three or four other young
officers (whom I knew not but came to know quite well) sat in
that railway carriage, proceeding by jerks, spaced out between
long waits, towards our destination. None of us had counted on
the journey taking so long or had had the sense to lay in food.
As it happened our improvidence was not visited too heavily upon
us. Sardines and gritty chocolate were on sale at the more important stations. But the lesson was not lost on any of us.

To watch the changing face of the countryside, the gradual
transformation from peace to war, was the chief interest of that
journey. As we travelled east the scars on the houses and villages
became more frequent: the movement of troops and military

transport more observable. By the afternoon of the succeeding day we were passing through country that, without being utterly devastated, was nevertheless disfigured and desolate. The booming of the guns was becoming more insistent. As darkness fell the flashes in the sky could be seen more plainly.

Our train meandered on.

My instructions told me that I was to report to the R.T.O. at the railhead—just that. Where the railhead was or how long it would take to reach, I had no idea. But as the evening wore on into night, we all felt that the journey must be nearing its end. If we went much farther we should strike the German lines!

Then, just as we were bracing ourselves to face another night in that carriage, the train drew in to what appeared to be a ruined factory.

'Is this it?' somebody asked.

'This is the railhead,' a voice replied.

'Where are we?'

'Albert.'

So. This was a place one had heard and read about in the papers. Albert—on the Somme.

We got out.

The station had been knocked about. There was little of it left except for the main walls which were badly battered.

The platform was crowded. Officers and men were bustling about, trying to find their way among the unlit ruins of the station. In the jostling and hubbub curses were mingled with laughter and an occasional greeting. The general movement was in the direction of a voice that was shouting at intervals, 'R.T.O.'s office this way!' Thither I too made my way.

The sorting of us took time. It was half an hour before I was able to report my name.

'Thomas...Thomas...' muttered the business-like R.T.O., as he ran his finger down the lists. 'Yes, here we are. 6th R.W.K. You'll be met here in the morning about eight. Next, please.'

I moved off. The time was half past one. Where and how should I pass the hours till eight? The platform was now clear, save for a few, like myself, who had nowhere to go.

Six and a half hours...

Strolling up to the end of the platform, I bumped into something that settled my problem—a pile of stacked stretchers. Setting one of them down on the ground I lay on it and passed a comfortable night.

IX

'Mr. Thomas, sir?'

I opened my eyes and found myself gazing at the benevolent, avuncular figure of a Battalion Sergeant-Major, who immediately saluted me.

I got up from my stretcher, shook myself and told the sergeant-major I was glad to see him.

He glanced at his watch.

'Eight o'clock,' he mused, rather as though he were speaking to himself. 'They'll just about be going over now.'

'Who will?' I asked.

'The battalion, sir.'

'Going over?'

'Yes, sir. Going over the top. Eight o'clock was zero hour for them this morning.'

'Oh.'

For the first time I experienced the sense of being, if not in the war, at all events very near it.

'Then I shall miss this particular attack...' I began, not sure of the impression I conveyed, or indeed whether, in the sergeant-major's presence, I ought to feel glad or sorry.

'And well out of it, too, sir, if you ask me,' observed the sergeant-major reassuringly. 'It'll be a dirty show, or I'm a Dutchman. This way, sir.'

He led the way out into the ruined streets of Albert and we started walking.

So. Twenty-four hours earlier and I might have been in the middle of a dirty show.*

---

* The sergeant-major, I discovered later, had been wrong in saying that zero hour was 8 a.m. The battalion actually went over at 1.45 p.m. Maybe the hour had been changed at the last moment. Another possibility is that the sergeant-major was trying to impress me.

'Tell me about it, sergeant-major.'

'Oh, I reckon it'll be the last show we'll be in down this way, for a time anyway,' he replied. 'We've had our fair share of it and the men need a rest now.'

'Been having a bad time lately?' I enquired.

'It hasn't been a picnic, sir, I'll say that. You've not been out before, sir, I think?'

'No, sergeant-major,' said I, feeling very like a new boy. 'This is my first time.'

'Just so, sir. Well, you're well out of today's show.'

'Where *is* the battalion? Near what place, I mean?'

'The Transport's at Montauban. It's a fair step, sir. Maybe a lorry'll give us a lift.'

We walked on. Presently, when we had got a little distance out of the town, the sergeant-major turned.

'There's the Madonna,' he said, pointing to the famous figure of the Virgin which had been knocked horizontal, but was still fixed to the top of the church steeple. 'The Madonna of Albert. It's strange how these things happen. There's another Madonna, standing in a graveyard just up near where we're going. All the other monuments have been blown to hell. But the Madonna isn't touched. It's queer to my way of thinking.'

All of a sudden I leapt into the air. Less than twenty yards away a heavy gun had been fired and the noise of the explosion nearly blew the breath out of my body.

The sergeant-major, when I next caught sight of him, was still contemplating the Madonna of Albert. Judging from his impassivity, you might have thought he was stone-deaf.

'That was some explosion,' I jerked out.

He turned towards me, and I detected a gleam of mischief in his eyes.

'Good many of those about in these parts,' he observed. And I wondered—but not for long—why he had chosen that particular spot to linger in.

We moved on.

Not having breakfasted I was feeling hungry. All I had on me was a packet of meat-essence cubes. I offered the sergeant-major one but he refused it. I think he regarded them as food for

small boys. Or else he didn't like the taste of them : and here I
would have agreed with him. Meat-essence cubes taken first
thing on an empty stomach are better than nothing. But not
much.

Ten minutes later a lorry lumbered up behind us and I was
glad of the lift.

X

'Here we are, sir. This is Montauban.'

'Montauban?' I repeated. 'Where?'

The sergeant-major smiled.

'Well, p'raps I should have said, sir, this *was* Montauban.'

The only two features of the place, as far as I could see, were
mud and shell-holes. Of buildings, even of ruined buildings, there
was not a trace. A few splintered stumps of trees showed where a
copse had been and here and there a patch of grass, sometimes
not more than a tuft, relieved the brownness of the landscape.
The rest was mud.

Parked a few hundred yards away from the spot where the
lorry had dropped us was the Battalion Transport— a collection
of army cookers, wagons, horses, mules and bell-tents. To one
of the latter I was guided by the sergeant-major who poked his
head in and announced my arrival to Mr. Hughes, the Transport
Officer. A sleepy voice bade me come in.

Mr. Hughes, obviously disturbed in his slumbers, greeted me
from his camp bed.

'Have you had any breakfast?' he yawned.

I said that I had not, whereupon he let out a peremptory roar
for one 'Silverside'. An answering shout was followed almost
immediately by the appearance of a villainous-looking face at
the tent flap.

'Get Mr. Thomas some breakfast,' commanded Mr. Hughes.
And with a 'Very good, sir,' the face of Silverside withdrew.

'Here, have a spot of this,' went on Mr Hughes, pouring some
brown liquid into an aluminium cup. For some reason I imagined
that he was offering me cold tea. One gulp told me I was wrong.
Mr. Hughes smiled at my convulsions.

'Haven't you had rum before?' he asked.

I shook my head and tried also to smile.

'You'd better finish it,' said Mr. Hughes. 'It'll do you good.'

A cup of rum has for the moment a heartening effect. As I stepped out of Hughes' tent the mud seemed friendlier, the scene of desolation less forbidding. My confidence rose. I was even bold enough to ask the orderly told off to show me to my tent if there was any news of the battalion—as if I had been following its fortunes for months.

'We 'aven't 'eard nothin' yet,' the man replied. 'I reckon they'll cop it, right enough.'

'Why?' I asked, feeling a peculiar interest in the show I was so narrowly missing.

'You can't do much in this mud, sir, 'cept get stuck in it. And Jerry's got hisself dug in by now.'

My instinct was to ask why, if that were so, an attack had been ordered at all. But I let it go.

I was—Hughes had told me—to be posted to a company whose commander was pointed out to me by the orderly as 'over in that shell-'ole, 'aving a bit of a wash'. At my approach a swarthy, saturnine face peered up at me out of the shell-hole. The body to which the head was attached wore no clothes and was being sluiced by its owner with water out of a green canvas bucket. It was the thinnest, most skeleton-like body I had ever seen.

'Captain Hodgson-Smith?' I said, saluting this lean and hairy form. Captain Hodgson-Smith grinned at me—as a skeleton should.

'Good morning,' he said. 'This is the first bath I've had for a month. I'll be out in a minute.'

His voice was soft, almost effeminate. It fell incongruously on its surroundings, yet there was a confidence in it that I found reassuring. I don't know why—and it sounds absurd—but his words and his manner of speaking reminded me of pre-war London, of hansom cabs, of tea at a restaurant after a matinée and then of the drive home to a flat in Baker Street. Curiously enough as soon as Hodgson-Smith had dressed and we had sat down to breakfast together, the first thing he asked me about was London.

When had I left there? How was the place looking? What shows were on? Was Joe Coyne as good as ever? What was the food like now at the Piccadilly? And so on. I did my best. But my knowledge of the West End was not extensive and my answers must have disappointed him.

'You live in London, of course?' he enquired.

I was glad to be able to say that I did. I felt that if I hadn't I would have sunk even lower in his estimation.

'It's the only place,' he observed, 'the only place in the world to live in. I've lived there all my life.'

I wondered what his age was. His swarthy complexion and deep-sunk brown eyes probably made him look older than he was. I put him at about thirty-five.

Presently he brought out his field note-book and said he might as well take some particulars, if I didn't mind.

Hodgson-Smith, I soon discovered, was a regular whale for particulars. He was a great believer in getting things down in black and white, preferably in duplicate or even in triplicate. One of his favourite occupations was checking his company list. His list was one of the most comprehensive documents of its kind that could ever have been compiled. It contained not only all the usual particulars of every man who had ever served in the company, but also such details as the full name and address in each case of the next-of-kin, notes of those who might suitably be promoted, and precise recommendations as to those N.C.O.s who should take over from others if the latter became casualties. The list was in triplicate—one copy in his own field book, one deposited in his valise, and one in the keeping of the second-in-command of the company. It constituted a master-key for the administration of the company. This passion of Hodgson-Smith's for detail and written statistics was, I learnt later, the source of great amusement throughout the battalion. Yet for all that there could have been few company commanders in France who knew and cared more about their men than did Hodge (as he was called) or earned the gratitude of their relatives as he must have earned it. For never a casualty occurred in his company but he wrote at once to the next-of-kin, giving the fullest possible particulars and in many cases forestalling the grim War Office telegram with a sympathetic letter. Into this path of virtue he guided all his subalterns.

'And who would you like me to write to, if you're knocked out?' he concluded. 'Your mother or your father?'

His matter-of-fact tone worried me a little. I had not been used to questions of that sort put with such directness. At home death was scarcely ever mentioned. When it was, you took care to wrap the subject up. Certainly the possibility of my being killed had never been referred to.

'I think my father, if you don't mind,' I said quietly.

It took me, I suppose, just about a week of Hodge's company to get used to his attitude towards death. It was an attitude, so far as one could tell, of utter indifference—not the indifference of a superman ready to sacrifice his life for a cause : but rather the natural indifference of a man who isn't interested. Life to Hodge was a job and so long as it lasted you got on with it. The thing to avoid was to outlast your usefulness and to live so long that you became an encumbrance to others. A short life on the whole was preferable. Once or twice I noticed that Hodge would become a trifle wistful about wanting to see a particular 'show' through. But this was rare. For the rest I never knew a man who showed so little interest in life apart from its routine, so little zest for living.

XI

The troops, Hodge told me, had been having a run for their money—or, as others said, 'the very devil of a time'. Since July the first, when the British had launched their great offensive on the Somme, the battalion had taken its full share of fighting. Now they were attacking a few kilometres away in front of Gueude- court.

'I wish they hadn't left me out,' Hodge said. He was in one of his wistful moods. 'They always seem to leave me out of the best shows.'

'Best?'

'Shows where there's some real fun. I never think a walk-over's much fun, you know.'

Hodge wasn't boasting or talking for effect. He meant what

he said. The truth was that he liked to be in the centre of serious activity. He liked also to feel that the burden was falling more heavily on him than on others.

'One feels, you know,' he said, 'that one isn't pulling one's weight.'

Hodge, I soon discovered, wasn't very popular, except with the senior officers of the battalion. His subalterns found him too conscientious and exacting. 'Off parade' for many of them meant total relaxation. In Hodge's view it meant nothing of the kind. Spare time, he held, should be devoted to 'making up for lost time'—visiting the men in their dug-outs or billets, holding conferences with the N.C.O.s, thinking out plans for increasing efficiency, and first, last and always keeping one's lists up to date.

Nor with the men was he very popular. For the sake of their well-being he never spared himself. Yet he lacked that quality of leadership which many less conscientious officers possessed. There was little or no magnetism in his personality. He was not the sort that men will follow to hell.

Not that his unpopularity worried him. What upset him more than anything was slackness, particularly administrative slackness, in his subalterns.

I suggested that if the battalion came badly out of this show somebody like him would be wanted to reorganise. This thought comforted him a little.

'Yes,' he replied, fixing me with his eye as though he saw in me a potential compiler of lists, 'yes, there is that. We're expecting a large new draft in a day or two. There'll be a lot of sorting out to do. We'll have to make new lists.'

The next night news came of the battalion's losses. Out of the five hundred who had gone into action two hundred came back. Of these two hundred only two were officers.

I had often read in the papers of heavy casualties. But I had never lain in the shadow of them as we all lay now. I was a newcomer and a stranger. But this one day's work of the enemy drew me closer to these men than weeks and months of peace-time soldiering could have done. Names which a few hours before meant nothing to me I found myself thinking of now with affection and with sorrow.

Forthwith the officers who had been left behind with the Transport were ordered to join the battalion. Hodge and I and half-a-dozen others went up. We left the Transport lines at Montauban just as dusk was falling, and headed by a guide we picked our way over the rough ground, skirting great shell craters, following sunken roads and filing through woods long since reduced to splintered tree-stumps. The boom of distant artillery formed a sombre background to the bursts of gunfire that broke from the hidden emplacements and camouflaged gun-pits scattered round us. At intervals the flare of Very lights lit up the scene ahead.

I trudged along behind Hodge in the semi-darkness. I was happy. I even felt exhilarated. A sense of expectancy hung in the air as when at the theatre the lights are lowered and all you can see is the glow on the curtain just before it rises. This, I assured myself, was what I had been waiting for : to be in France and 'going up the line'. For all that anyone could have offered me I would not have been in any other place.

'How far,' I asked the fellow behind me, 'are we from the front line?'

'God knows,' he grunted. He was an older hand than I was and less enthusiastic.

We trudged on. Parties of men loomed up and disappeared. Sentries challenged us and bade us pass. Lights flared and far away machine guns rattled.

XII

Our arrival caused no stir. The men had had a gruelling time and desired nothing but to be withdrawn from the line and allowed to rest. Most of them were lying in shell-holes which had been hastily linked together by a trench, the whole being dignified by the name of the Reserve Line. Two hundred men there were : and as the platoons had been reduced to less than skeleton strength, the battalion had been divided into two groups, of one of which Hodge now took command. It was like him, as I came to know well, never to let the idea that men needed rest stand in the way of a job that had to be done. Himself he never spared :

his men he spared as often as he could. But when essential work was to be done the men had to do it so long as life was in them. And now a job was waiting: a communication trench had to be dug and dug quickly, while the darkness lasted, linking the Reserve with the Support Line. Fifty men were told off, and I was put in charge: my first job in the line—and nearly my last. For as we were out digging a random bullet struck the man working next to me and laid him out. Stretcher bearers took him off. What became of him I never heard. But he took the bullet that so nearly came to me.

As we bent at our digging, my spade struck a spongy thing that both resisted and gave, a thing whose size and substance puzzled me.

'What,' I said to the sergeant, 'can this be?'

The sergeant bent down in the dark and gave the thing a jab with his spade. Then he stepped back and cleared his throat.

'Better dig round 'im, sir,' he advised.

Early that morning the rain started and continued without break for two whole days. Shell-holes and trenches were flooded and on the third day we were glad enough to be relieved, even though it meant going back to the muddy area that had been Montauban.

XIII

As the adjutant at Etaples had told me, the Colonel was known as 'The Fire-eater'. The nickname suited him. Picture a man of middle height, clean-shaven, without an ounce of surplus flesh, an eye as clear as a crystal, a tongue as sharp as a razor and a command of language that a sailor would have envied. Whatever other faults the Colonel had, he was without vice of hesitation. No one could have called him a ditherer. He never left you guessing: in conversation as in action, he went directly to the point. Toughness was all: and when we were out of the line he saw to it that neither officers nor men lacked opportunities for strengthening their fibre. A favourite game of his, particularly when new officers joined the battalion, was to hold a riding ring. The officers who couldn't ride were given the liveliest mounts: and the Colonel, standing in the middle of the ring, had fun forcing the pace with his whip and telling the tyros where, so to speak, they got off.

Luckily I never met the full force of his personality. When I joined the battalion I was too junior for him to take much notice of (I had already learnt to ride and passed his test without mishap) and at the end of my first month he was given a Brigade and left us. But his name and his methods were not forgotten, though their fame was soon to be eclipsed by the man who took his place as our C.O.

Wililam Robert Aufrère Dawson was twenty-seven when he became Colonel of our battalion. No man I have ever met was more suited by nature to be a commanding officer : no man succeeded in his job more magnificently than he did. Let me try to give you a picture of Bob Dawson. Imagine a tall, square-shouldered, gracefully proportioned man, whose jaw warns you that if you are going to disagree with him you had better choose your moment and also find a pretty solid reason in your favour. For he was a man of moods and uncertain temper. A stray injudicious word would send him flying off the handle. I have heard him heap unprintable abuse, for no adequate reason, on an officer—and that, too, on parade. I have seen him pick up a man by the scruff of the neck and throw him down into the bottom of the trench, simply because the chap was a recruit and did not know the name of his company commander. In London once I was walking along the pavement with him and his mother (each was intensely proud of the other) when a passing stranger accidentally brushed against her. In an instant Dawson had got the fellow by the shoulder and was giving him the kind of dressing-down that might have led to trouble. Violent qualities like these do not always command respect. But Dawson got away with them mainly because of his other qualities.

First, he knew his job. A regular for only six months before the war, he had an instinctive grasp of soldiering. Before joining the army he had been to Oxford, and perhaps for that reason had a wider outlook than those whose training had been purely military. Casualties were partly responsible for the speed of his promotion : but he would not have been given command of a battalion at twenty-seven had he not also been endowed with

peculiar qualities of leadership. Besides knowing his job he was
personally brave. By the end of the war he had a right to wear
at least six wound stripes on his sleeve and to his D.S.O. three
bars. These were the outward signs of his courage. Once when a
position had to be defended at all costs and repeated onslaughts
had thinned the ranks of the battalion, Dawson strolled calmly
along the parapet, in front of his men and in full view of the
Germans, taking his pipe out of his mouth now and then to say
a word of encouragement to his men or to crack a joke. The pipe,
one felt, was a stroke of genius. Sometimes he was more foolhardy
than he should have been. A Colonel has no business to go out
on patrol in no-man's land. But before a raid it was Dawson's
habit 'to have a look round', which meant that he would creep
out in front, preferably alone, slithering along on his belly, to
see, for example, that the barbed wire had been properly smashed
by the gunners so that his men should be able to get through. If
by chance the gunners had not done their job, they would hear
about it from him—at first hand. Rarely can a C.O. have been
so reckless and foolhardy—or have commanded such devotion
from his men.

Dawson had no more respect for Authority than Authority
deserved. He had a quick eye for incompetence, especially in
high places.

Fools he never suffered gladly : fools with red tabs and gold
braid (in Dawson's language 'velvet-arsed buggers') he suffered
not at all. Knowledge that 'the old man' could and did stand up
to brass hats strengthened the hold that he had on all of us. We
knew that whatever anyone 'up top' might do, Dawson would
never let us down.

From his officers he expected as much as he gave—which was
everything. For the lazy and incompetent he showed his contempt by getting rid of them as soon as possible. There were in
those days several ways of getting rid of undesirables. You could
send them on a course, which would be the first step towards
drafting them on to a specialist job : you could make them into
Town Majors : you could detail them to some liaison work of
one sort or another. Or of course you could mark them down
for the stickier jobs in the line. If Dawson favoured one method

more than another it was probably the last. Nor did it profit you
much to go sick. In Erewhon a man convicted of illness was regarded as a criminal and punished accordingly. To say that
Dawson shared that view would be an exaggeration. But to plead
sick was not the surest way to open the flood-gates of the Colonel's
sympathy.

Dawson used to call himself a Royalist. His favourite question,
when a newly-joined officer was introduced to him, was: 'Are
you a Royalist or a filthy Roundhead?' That was the atmosphere
in which he lived and out of which he had never emerged. To
me his opinions were, to say the least, challenging: and when
I knew him better I had many arguments with him. 'Tonight,'
I wrote home in October, 1918, 'I'm going to dinner with the
Colonel. I had a terrific argument with him the other night from
10.0 till 2.0 a.m.! He is really hunnish in his views ("Might is
right: survival of the fittest", etc.).' I recall the argument. It took
place in a cellar at Henin-Liétard during the great advance. The
end of the war was in sight and we were discussing the kind of
peace that would be made and the treatment that ought to be
meted out to the Germans. His view was that they should be
kept in permanent subjection ('Hold the buggers down by
force!') I was ignorant of politics, but had been brought up in
a vaguely liberal atmosphere. I had been to one or two Liberal
party meetings at election times and my father had always voted
Liberal. I suppose this, coupled with a natural joy in argument,
was the reason why I took the opposite line to the Colonel's. A
world, I felt, run on Dawson's lines—at least the lines he suggested to me in that cellar—was not the kind of world I was
looking forward to living in.

But the truth was that his personality overpowered me. I might
argue with him and be convinced in my mind that his way was
wrong. But so far as behaviour and action were concerned, I was
under his thumb. Even a glance from him would do for me. For
Dawson's glance was more eloquent than words. It told you that
deep down there was confidence between himself and you—or
at least he assumed there was. Coming from Dawson such an
assumption was too flattering to be resisted. So great was his
influence on me that had he lived I might after the war have

stayed in the army. For he had the impression—proof of the un-soundness of his judgment—that I had the makings of a soldier in me: and towards the end of 1918 it was all but understood between us that I would continue in the Service. This under-standing caused me great uneasiness. I used to wonder how on earth I was going to get out of it. There was always the chance that I might be killed or seriously wounded. Short of that I felt there was no hope for me. Either I should have to stay on in the army or else I should have to let Dawson down. And that, in those days, was unthinkable.

The question worried me. But it never occurred to me that the answer would be found in Dawson's own death. I never believed in a man bearing 'a charmed life'. If I had, I should have put Dawson high on the list. So, I think, would most of the battalion. For when you were with Dawson you felt safe. Often I walked by his side along the stickiest of roads and through the unhealthiest of trenches, and because he was with me I did not feel afraid. Had I been alone, I could scarcely have dared to creep along even on all fours. But he would stride ahead, with his pipe in his mouth, as confidently as if he had been walking down Bond Street. (As a matter of fact, he would never have been seen in Bond Street with a pipe on: his 'West End' standards would have seen to that.) Did he know what fear was? I often wond-ered. Then one day, in 1917, I came across him alone. Our lines were being heavily bombarded and I was going along my sector to see if the men were all right. Turning into one of the bays, I ran into Dawson. He was standing in an odd position: instead of leaning with his back to the side of the trench, he was standing facing it, gripping the mud wall with crooked fingers. His ex-pression was drawn, as though he were in pain. On seeing me, he relaxed and tried to laugh. It was the laugh of a nervous, fright-ened man. I gazed at him, wondering what had happened. For a moment I thought he might have been wounded.

'Are you hit, sir?' I asked.

'*Hit?*' He repeated the word as though he did not know what I meant. Then he went on: 'I suppose it's never occurred to you that I could be frightened?' He was looking at me squarely and had got possession of himself again. I said the idea had never occurred to me.

'Do you think I like these bloody bombardments,' he went on. I told him that I didn't think that, either, but that I had never seen him afraid.

'Well, you have now,' he observed. 'It was because I was afraid that I was clinging to this bloody trench.'

'I don't blame you,' I said. 'I'm frightened myself.'

'But when I'm with other people,' he said, 'I don't show the fear I feel, that's all. Nor do you have to, either.'

'No, sir,' I said, feeling proud that he should seem to place me in the same category as himself : that is, the category of the really brave who feel afraid but do not show it.

'But I don't mind telling you now——' he added, but evidently thought better of it, for he broke off and with a gruff, 'Come on', led the way along the trench in his usual confident way. And, walking behind him, I felt safe.

Well, that was Dawson—or some idea of him, at least.

XIV

For months after leaving the Somme we lay in a quiet sector of the line just south of Arras. A week in the front line, a week in reserve and a week in billets—that was the routine. It was for me a comfortable way of getting used to the western front. Instead of coming up against the war with a bump, one slid into it.

The trenches had been well built and our main work was to keep them in repair. Our time was spent in sandbag-revetting and laying or re-laying duck-boards. Every day Hodge would inspect the trenches, using his little cane to tap the particular sandbags which seemed to him to have been badly placed or the particular duck-boards which were not as firmly laid as they should have been. The platoon commander concerned would take careful note of his criticisms, because Hodge had a memory for detail and it went badly with any of us if next day he found that the faults he had noticed had not been corrected. It was an odd war, I felt, in which our chief concern was not to fight, but to see that the holes in the ground we occupied were kept as spick and span as we could make them.

Occasional excitement came our way, as when the Boche celebrated 'stand-to' at dawn by lobbing over some trench-mortars. Ungainly great things they were as we watched them turning over in the air and wondered where they were going to land. As often as not you misjudged the trajectory and found yourself running towards the spot where they burst. These 'minnies' on the whole did little harm. They would scarcely ever fall in the trench and even if they did the chances were heavily against that particular bay being occupied.

Only once during our period there did one of them find its mark. It fell within a few feet of the cubby-hole which my platoon sergeant had made his headquarters. There were two men sitting with him at the time. Half-an-hour or so beforehand I had been there chatting with them. The cubbyhole was roofed over with corrugated iron, enough to stop a splinter but no proof against a direct hit. I had seen the explosion and felt that it could not be very far away from Sergeant Young's place. I went along and, as I was going, I heard a call, soon to become familiar and one that always filled me with foreboding—'Stretcher-bearers!' I hurried on. The crater which the mortar had made was just at the back of Young's cubby-hole. The cubby-hole itself had been blown in and its occupants buried. Spades were fetched and four of us started digging like mad. The acrid smell of the explosive reeked in our nostrils and we had to keep low for fear of drawing fire. I suppose we must have dug for a quarter of an hour—though it seemed much longer—before we came upon Young's leg. We hoped that he might be lying so that he could breathe. We dug carefully now. But we were too late. His mouth, I noticed, was open and full of earth. Buried near him were two other bodies. These were the first dead bodies I had ever seen. . . .

Besides these 'minnie' strafes, there were two other forms of excitement. One was night wiring in no-man's land and the other night patrols. The patrol provided the greater test of nerves but the wiring was, I think, less safe. The main things to remember when you went out wiring were not to make too much noise and to keep still, whatever your position, when a Very light went up.

The effect was sometimes grotesque, because as soon as the light went up you remained stock still—your arms might be stretched out, you might be crouching or standing at full height, but whatever your position you held it. I sometimes thought that a party of men caught so must have looked like figures on the Parthenon frieze—well, something like them.

The first time I went out I pictured myself slithering about from one shell-hole to another and not daring to stand up. But once I had stood up, confidence returned. After a time wiring became a boring occupation. Not so patrols. Nothing much happened on any of my patrols, but the feeling that at any moment something might keep you up to scratch. A patrol consisted usually of an officer and a sergeant or maybe a corporal. The object would be to find out what the enemy's wire was like, whether a particular trench or sap was manned, or to discover generally if anything was doing.

The preliminaries were stimulating. First you emptied your pockets of everything that might disclose your identity. For the same reason you removed all regimental badges. You saw to it that you were not carrying anything that might reflect a light. Your bayonet would be dulled, usually by having a sock drawn over it. Finally you blackened your face with burnt cork. Having thus washed yourself out, so to speak, you were ready to 'move off' (you always 'moved off' in the army: you never 'went'). Scrambling over the parapet always gave one a kick. You were never quite sure that you wouldn't be greeted with machine-gun fire. Taking your bearings you made for the gap in the wire. You knew where it was and could usually get there 'at the crouch'. But once you were through, there was no standing up. You moved off 'at the slither'. And then the fun—if you can call it that—began. Every object seemed to take on human shape. If you gazed at it long enough, you could swear that it was moving. Often you stalked a tree-stump or even a lump of earth, believing it to be a German. Not until a Very light went up, lighting the whole scene, would you see what a fool you were making of yourself. Nearing the German lines one might (or might not) catch some sound of the enemy—a voice, a footfall, the metallic sound of a rifle being shifted, or maybe only a cough or the clearing of a throat. Hearing noises like these, you kept very still. Even then you might find that what you had been listening to was nothing but the sound of loose wire blowing in the wind.

So you slithered about no-man's land, not knowing what you might come up against from a dead body to an enemy patrol. The operation sounds more fearsome than it was, especially when you had a good, reliable sergeant with you. There was also the feeling—an appeal here to one's vanity—that everyone on the company front had been warned that you were out. You were, as well as being in the dark, also in the limelight.

XV

Our company headquarters dug-out in this sector of the line was only a few steps below ground. (On our left, where the soil was chalky, the dugouts were much deeper, some of them thirty or forty feet down). Here we eat, drank, slept, talked, censored letters, drew up our plans for work and, under Hodge's eagle eye, saw to it that our lists were up-to-date. The furniture was simple—an upturned crate for a table, candles stuck in empty whisky bottles for a light, the luxury of wire-beds to sleep upon, and a backless chair which Hodge occupied while the rest of us sat on the edges of the beds. The clammy atmosphere and earthy smell of the place hit you as you came in from the upper air: but you quickly absorbed it and it ceased to trouble you. More irksome were the rats, which were large and greedy and for the most part tame. They never failed to appear when food was about (as it was during most of the day) and took their exercise by crawling over you at night. At one period a cat who was a fine ratter attached itself to our headquarters. This cat was very welcome and we did all we could to encourage it to stay. The best thing of all was to induce the cat to choose your particular bunk to sleep in; the rats would then keep clear. Sometimes I would pot at these rats with my revolver in the dug-out (the only use I ever had for my revolver) and Hodge would tell me in a dull, monotonous tone to be careful not to hit the whisky bottle. It was typical of Hodge that he should warn me about the whisky rather than about himself. When I remarked on the fact, his explanation was characteristic : 'If you hit me I at least shan't mind about the whisky : but if you hit the whisky we shall all be in the soup.' As a matter of fact on no occasion did I hit either the whisky or the rats. But Hodge continued to keep an eye on me —even in his sleep : or so it seemed; for he was the only man I ever met who slept with his eyes open. It was a strange experience (until one got used to it) to light the candle in the dug-out and see Hodge asleep in his bunk, gazing at you with a fixed, unwinking stare.

Out of the trenches, you were either right out—that is, in a village miles behind the line : or else you were in close reserve— that is, in a more or less battered and uninhabited village immediately behind the front. The latter billet was slap-up compared with the trenches. There might not be a roof to the house, and the walls might be gaping, but iron bedsteads could be scrounged and the odd bits of furniture that remained gave life a civilised background, the more so as the mess servants made the most of every piece they found. Did the room sport a sideboard, the mess crockery (made of tin) was promptly displayed on it. If the dustbin was found to contain a picture, it was duly hung on the wall. The greatest find of all would be a piano. In one of my letters home I told how some of the lads in our company had managed to bring two pianos from a neighbouring village. The one destined for the officers' mess was larger than the entrance to the vault in which we happened to be living. 'Nothing daunted,' I wrote, 'the boys set to work with hammers and axes and by dint of much pushing and shoving and hammering, managed to get the instrument inside. It was filled with brickdust and several notes were missing—to say nothing of the outer woodwork which was considerably damaged. But all that didn't matter a bit. The men had got the piano in and that satisfied them. That it would be no use for playing on afterwards didn't seem to occur to them!'

But if billets of this kind were slap-ups, the real billets in the villages behind the line were very heaven. Feather mattresses, sheets, a bedroom to yourself, hot baths in a tub, every kind of delicacy for the table—what more could one desire? The answer, so far as I was concerned, was privacy and solitude. In the crowd

I was with—which was much the same as any other crowd—
you were considered odd if you 'went off on your own'. The
natural thing was to knock round with your companions and do
what they were doing. Even reading was looked upon as highbrow. To be discovered reading a book of poems was to risk
the charge of lunacy. Among the books I took in my valise to
France were the Rubáiyát of Omar Khayyam and a small Greek
anthology. These, had they ever come to light, would have been
enough to convict me without a hearing. But I took care not to
display them and read them only when I was alone.

It was in one of these billets-behind-the-line that we had the
luck to spend Christmas. The day was celebrated with as much
cheeriness and home atmosphere as we could bring to it. The men
had their 'blow-out' in the middle of the day, and in the evening
our company staged a sing-song. I was in charge of the entertain-
ment side of this affair, while another officer looked after the
refreshments. The sing-song was held in an empty barn which
flanked the courtyard of our billet (is 'courtyard' the right word?
the place was nothing but a dump for midden). A stage was rig-
ged up, a piano acquired, and rows of benches were borrowed
from the local school. The show went off, as such shows normally
do, with a good many unpremeditated twists from the performers
and a good deal of generosity from the audience. I do not remember anything about the show except that the French farmer's
wife on whom we were billeted sat with members of her family
in the front row and was not, so far as one could tell from her
expression, very much impressed by the performance. I remember
too that I recited 'A Ballad of John Nicholson', and I only
remember that because the following lines occur in it:

> Take off, take off those shoes of pride
> Carry them whence they came.

This verse became a stock joke in our mess. When you came in
from field exercises with your trench boots covered with mud,
Hodge would solemnly order you to 'take off those shoes of
pride and carry them whence they came'.

The one shadow which fell across our festivities that Christmas was caused by the sudden death of Clarence Budd. He had

gone down sick a week or so before and the next we heard of
him was that he had died of cerebro-spinal meningitis. Budd had
improved on acquaintance at the front. He was never communi-
cative: but the indifference he showed for his surroundings and
to his own fate became more marked: and that gave the men
a measure of confidence in him which in turn seemed to sweeten
his own character, or at all events to take the edge off his morose-
ness. But he was a queer, lone chap and none of us knew him at
all intimately.

XVI

On the day after Christmas I was given command of a company. Its previous commander had been a *locum tenens* for its
real commander who was at home recovering from a wound.
This *locum* had proved himself a failure; and one of the first
things Dawson did on taking over the battalion was to devise a
means of getting rid of him. This having been done, Dawson—on
Hodge's recommendation—put me in his place. The C.O.'s instructions were brief: 'B company's the worst in the battalion.
I want it to be the best. Get on with it.'

My sudden elevation was due mainly to the losses which the
battalion had sustained on the day that I had joined them. I
was not made a captain, and it was indicated very clearly to me
that my command of B company would last only until I ceased
to give satisfaction or until its rightful commander returned—
whichever of those two events might happen first. As Hodge and
the Adjutant told me—this was my chance.

Having mentioned the Adjutant I must say a word about him:
for he was a 'character'. His name was Alderman, and he was
a ranker. Soldiering had been his profession. He wore the South
African ribbon (and the D.S.O.) and talked to soldiers in language they could understand. There were several ranker officers
in our battalion, all of them unpopular with the men—mainly
because they knew their job and there was no chance of 'swinging it over them'. But Alderman, though he was not universally
popular, was universally respected. There was a directness of
attack about him that appealed to everyone. Subtlety and sar-
casm (which all men hate in their officers) were not in his make-

up, and though the men knew that they might not be treated
very politely by Alderman they knew also that they would be
treated fairly. He was a good administrator, particularly of rough
justice. He was a splendid lieutenant and interpreter of orders.
And he was a loyal friend. Where he fell short was in his conversation, which was boring, and in the reckless way he exposed
himself to danger.

To spend an evening with Alderman was to be subjected to
endless reminiscences mostly about his early days of soldiering.
A few of the anecdotes were interesting enough, but even his best
were hardly worth repeating—a fact which everybody recognised
except Alderman himself, who told the same stories over and
over again. It was often said that Alderman's conversation was
amusing to listen to only when it was directed at a third party.
To eavesdrop on some of his altercations with the battalion
pioneer corporal could be a treat. The corporal, whose name was
Hart, was also an old soldier—so old that he occupied a privileged position. More licence was permitted to Hart by the officers
than to any other N.C.O. in the battalion, not excluding the
battalion sergeant-major. In other days he would have qualified
as King's Jester. In Alderman Corporal Hart recognised one of
his own kidney and the two talked to one another—and often
argued—as equals. One of Hart's duties was to paint the White
Horse—the regimental badge—on our tin helmets. Alderman
would often pull him up for his slowness at the job. Here is a
sample of the kind of conversation you might hear between
Alderman and Hart—neither of whom had an 'h' in his vocabu-
lary:

''Allo, 'Art, 'ow about them 'elmets?'

'Wot 'elmets?'

As Alderman had omitted the 'Corporal', Hart felt entitled to
omit the 'sir'.

'The 'elmets you was goin' to paint the white 'orses on.'

'Well, 'aven't I painted 'alf-a-dozen of 'em?'

''Alf-a-dozen! I thought I said you was to paint a 'undred.'

'A 'undred! 'Ow can I paint a 'undred in 'alf-an-hour?'

'Alf-an-hour! You've 'ad a 'ole day to paint 'em in!'

'A 'ole day?'

'Wot was you doin' all yesterday?'

'Working on D company's cooker.'

'And since when did D company's cooker take precedure of them white 'orses I told you to paint on the 'elmets?'

And so on—more like two back-chat comedians than corporal and captain.

Alderman's recklessness in face of danger was due, not to bravado, but to a genuine desire to be 'first there' at the centre of the show. He hated to be on the fringe of anything, and when he became adjutant and his post during an action was at battalion headquarters Dawson was often hard put to it to prevent him from dodging off up to one of the companies or even up to the foremost platoon, 'just to see 'ow things are goin', sir.' (Not that Dawson himself set a good example—as Alderman was quick to point out). When at the end of 1917 Alderman, then a major and Dawson's second-in-command, led the battalion into action at Cambrai, we all of us knew what the end of it would be.

But to revert. The early days of 1917 I spent in making myself an infernal nuisance to my new company. Everyone from the officers downwards had fallen into a state of slackness and indifference. Outwardly the company presented a slovenly appearance. Behind the scenes the day-to-day routine was no less slovenly. The situation called for masterful handling, for a leader who had confidence in himself and the capacity for inspiring confidence in others, who was indifferent to unpopularity and at the same time could command men's loyalty. Looking at it squarely I could not think of anyone less suited to the job than I was. Nor did the fact that most of the officers, N.C.O.s and men in the company had been with the battalion much longer than I had make the job any easier.

However, at twenty one can take on anything. When, under the rule of military discipline as enforceable on active service, one's word is law, even a diffident, yet slightly obstinate character may assume the appearace of strength. Moreover I knew that I could always count on Hodge for advice and encouragement. I knew too that Dawson would back me.

I tackled the problem in two ways. On the one hand I imposed

a kind of Prussian discipline. A year previously, I remembered,
the adjutant of the reserve battalion at Crowborough had
attended a course of drill at Chelsea barracks and had come back
full of the theory that the foundation of all discipline was drill.
In order to hand on the benefits of his experience he had put
the junior officers (of whom I had been one) through such a
course of barrack square drill as none of us was likely to forget.
This was the course of drill that I now inflicted on the N.C.O.s
of my company. Every afternoon at half past two I assembled
them in a field well off the road and surrounded by trees so that
we could not be overlooked. Here I marched them up and down,
halted them, stood them to attention for periods on end, searching the ranks for the slightest movement, and in general made
myself so unpleasant that I have no doubt many of them longed
for the time when they would return to the peace and quiet of
the trenches. In this Draconian treatment I had an ally in the
company sergeant-major, an old soldier who, like the rest, had
relapsed into slackness when there had been no pressure from
above. Under the new regime his spirit revived. Ancient memories
crowded back—memories of peace-time soldiering when the
army *was* the army and not a collection of civilians dressed up
in uniform. The result was that he and I were regarded by the
company as a couple of unholy terrors, whose mission was to think
up new devices for making life as uncomfortable as possible.

Nor when the whole company was on parade did I forbear
to curse them in the mass, or to make them go through the same
movements again and again until I was satisfied. And this I learnt
—that so long as your curses were hurled at men in the mass
there was no bad feeling. The fatal thing was to single out a
particular N.C.O. or man by name. That always caused resentment.

My other way of tackling the problem was less conventional.
I made an appeal to *esprit de corps*, this time not in the mass,
but individually. On these occasions I would adopt the man-to-
man attitude—talking like a father to fellows twice my age. A
particularly bad case would be brought before me at Orderly
Room. Instead of at once inflicting the maximum penalty or
sending him on to the C.O.'s Orderly Room, I would suddenly

clear the court, telling everybody to leave, even including the sergeant-major—much to the latter's astonishment and, I think, disgust. Then I would talk to the man and try to appeal to his better feelings (how he must have hated me—though I didn't think so at the time). I would tell him that he belonged to the finest company in the battalion and so on (a lot he must have cared!) and in exchange for letting him off this time I would ask for his assurance for the future...

What these men thought of my pi-jaws I have no idea. Looking back now I can guess. 'Trying to work 'is public-school ways on to us,' was the way they would have put it. And small blame to them. What could they have cared for belonging to the 'finest' company? Had they been soldiers an appeal to the 'glorious traditions of the regiment' might have got them (as a matter of fact the 'glorious traditions' did find a reference in my 'pi-jaws'). But they were not soldiers. They were, as the sergeant-major never tired of pointing out, civilians in uniform—just as I myself was a schoolboy in uniform. All they wanted was to win the war and go back home as soon as possible.

Did my Prussianism-cum-pi-jaws have any effect? I think they did. One man stabbed himself in the leg with his bayonet. But he was a man who should never have been in a fighting unit at all. He lived his life in a mortal funk, and I suppose the time came when he couldn't stand it any longer and preferred to risk the penalties of a self-inflicted wound to doing another stretch in the line. My methods were doubtless the last straw, but the chap would never have made a fighter or been the slightest use in battle. So far as the company and the war were concerned, it was just as well he left us. But apart from him and one or two inveterate grousers the situation certainly improved.

My own particular trouble was with the officers. It was not that they failed to support me—though one or two of them were obviously luke-warm. But it was difficult for us in our day-to-day dealings to break through a formality of manner for which my attitude towards the company was responsible. I was regarded as a strange being whose one idea was to jerk people into activity and to make life even more unpleasant than it was already. Also I was unreliable. No one quite knew when I might erupt. Consequently my colleagues tended to be on their guard—which was a bar to easy relationship. I had, as I said, Hodge to go to. I could discuss anything with him. But he had his own cares and could not be expected to burden himself with mine as well. Besides this, for all his friendliness, Hodge was too matter-of-fact, too cynical, almost too saturnine a person, to share the emotions of friendship. He was much older than I was and in the early days at all events his friendliness was tinged with an avuncular quality wihch limited our intercourse.

I was not lonely. But in my four months with the battalion I had made no particular friend. There was no one—like Dunn —who had a life outside soldiering, and with whom one could laugh. I often thought of Dunn and missed him.

Then one morning early in February 1917 Gilbert Carré walked into the billet.

PART THREE

IN MEMORIAM

I HAD HEARD OF Carré, but only vaguely. There had been talk of him in the mess, and of his twin brother Meyrick. The two of them had been among the earliest officers in the battalion. Gilbert had been wounded on the Somme the previous July, and Meyrick, I gathered, had been hit at Gueudecourt on the day of my arrival. Meyrick's name would crop up when someone had been forgetful or absent-minded—'just like Carré', they would say. And those who knew him would smile and as often as not go off into some reminiscence of Meyrick's absent-mindedness.

Gilbert, possibly because he was less absent-minded than his twin, had left behind him no distinctive memories. 'Gilbert Carré? Yes, he was Meyrick's brother. Meyrick was the absent-minded one, you know. I remember once...' In the stories of Meyrick's forgetfulness Gilbert was forgotten.

Now he had turned up again.

His arrival had no meaning for me at the time; but I remember the occasion of it very clearly. We were in billets—the usual small farm-house—and had just finished breakfast. I had been out (at the bottom of the garden stood a neat canvas-covered erection, confirming the suspicions of the French that we were a nation of sanitary enthusiasts) and when I came back I found a young man I had not seen before in the mess. He was standing with his back to the sunlight which poured in through the curtained window and was talking to Hibbert, the shoe-maker corporal who had been commissioned from the ranks. Hibbert was still sitting at the breakfast table.

'Hullo, skipper,' he said, when I appeared. 'This is Carré. Used to be in the company.'

Rather to my surprise—and certainly to Hibbert's who now that he was an officer made a point of all-being-pals-together in the mess—Carré saluted. It was a punctilious act and rather clumsily performed.

Carré was of medium height and of lightish build. He had fair hair and blue eyes and his voice, like his manner, was gentle and diffident.

'I was wondering, sir,' I heard him saying to me, 'if I might take over my old platoon—number 6?'

There was something ridiculous in my being called 'sir' by a man who had been wounded in action before I had even arrived in France. (For the matter of that I have never been able to feel entirely unselfconscious on being called 'sir' by anybody.) I couldn't help smiling. His salute and his formal manner of address were very much in line with the kind of discipline I had been trying to instil into the company. Yet the spectacle of Gilbert Carré solemnly performing in front of me brought out the absurd side of this kind of relationship between one man and another. I had the sense, even at this first meeting with him, that he and I were play-acting with one another: he pretending to be a keen subaltern and I pretending to be a rather exacting company commander. So unreal were these attitudes that I was conscious of detachment from them. I was, as it were, watching the play through the eyes of a third person. Just as I had heard him asking me a question, so I heard myself making a reply. I was telling him that number 6 platoon was his.

From the day of Carré's arrival I became conscious of him, as of no one else in the battalion. The pleasure his presence gave me was known to no one else, least of all to him. Being innately fearful of showing my feelings, particularly of seeming to accord him any favour in preference to the other officers in the company, I was often more critical of him than was necessary. I would remark to him on the slovenly appearance of some of his men or on the untidiness of their billets. My tone would be solemn rather than wrathful. When he took my remarks to heart, as he always did, I wanted to laugh.

The curious thing was that even off duty, even in the relaxation of the mess, I found myself behaving awkwardly towards him. I had the impression that he, like his brother Meyrick, was an intellectual. Concerning Meyrick I had heard the most stupendous things—that he had been a scholar at Balliol, that he was reading for his Doctorate of Philosophy, and heaven knows what else. Gilbert, for all I knew, took after him. At all events he had a scholarly appearance—which was more than any of the rest of us had—and though he showed no outward signs of being a highbrow, yet I could not help feeling that the conversation round our mess table was not much to his taste. This feeling—quite unjustified and, as it turned out, very wide of the mark—showed itself in my awkward behaviour.

All of which resulted in his tending to avoid my company. When he could not avoid it, he showed such a marked respect for me that instead of our becoming friends we were developing merely into superior and subordinate, which was not only painful, but ridiculous.

One day, after he had been with us about three weeks, I asked him to come for a walk. I wanted to straighten things out. The invitation was not easily given because I was not easy in my own mind on what I could do to straighten them out. At present he respected me—because he did not know me and also because I was his company officer. If he got to know me, he might easily lose his respect for me and come to dislike me.

Gilbert seemed surprised when I asked him, but he accepted— probably because he felt he ought to.

So I took the first of many walks with him.

I asked him how he thought the company compared with what it had been in his day.

'I admire tremendously the hold you have over it,' he said.

This answer was so astonishing and unexpected that I thought I had misheard him.

'The hold I have over it?' I repeated.

'The sense of discipline there is.'

Was he, I wondered, trying to flatter me?

'The company had got slack,' I said shortly, 'and we had to pull it together, that's all. The trouble is, everyone seems to have taken it too seriously.'

It was not a fair remark so far as the company was concerned, because no one had taken the drill and the discipline more seriously than I had.

It was Gilbert's turn to be surprised.

'You speak as if you hadn't taken it very seriously yourself,' he said.

'Well, what do you think?'

'I think you take everything very seriously. You seem too, anyway.'

'Keeping up appearances...'

'Not always,' Gilbert suggested. 'Not in the mess. Why trouble in the mess?'

'I suppose I can't help it. There doesn't seem anyone...'

'Anyone what?'

'Well, anyone to joke with. Besides, they think I'm a nuisance. That's what Dawson meant me to be.'

'Dawson,' remarked Gilbert, with deliberation, 'doesn't think much of me.'

'Why do you say that?'

'He doesn't like weak people like me. He likes people to be strong and executive...like you.'

If I had not felt ashamed, I should have laughed.

'Good God!' I said. 'If he only knew!'

I then tried to give Gilbert an idea of the way I felt, of the doubts I had, of the diffidence which in these months I had tried hard to conceal, and of the sense of absurdity, even of frivolity, which would keep intertwining itself with what was supposed to be a seriousness of purpose. I found myself talking as easily and freely to Gilbert as if I had known him all my life. In doing that I felt not only a sense of relief, as a man does when he meets someone who will share a burden, but also a feeling of great happiness, as a man does when he had found a sympathetic friend. Henceforth the business (as Gilbert put it) of standing on my dignity and of adhering to the rules of military discipline was lightened for me by the knowledge, shared between us, that the whole great tragedy in which we had our tiny parts to play was best interpreted as comedy.

11

Those two months—February and March—we spent in field

training, far behind the line. In January we had been up to Arras for a spell. A queer experience that—an amazing blend of civilisation and desolation. For billets we used maisonettes and sometimes wealthy-looking mansions : only there was no glass in any of the windows and as often as not the walls and ceilings were gashed with ugly rents. Such furniture as had been left was usually of the solid, immovable kind : a vast mahogany table would be in position in the dining *salon*, and placed round it for the evening meal would be not chairs, but packing cases. In the bedrooms splendid bedsteads appeared ready to receive us—but it was impossible to lie in them because they had no springs or slats. But the oddest thing of all about Arras was the change that came on the city when darkness fell. By day Arras was a city of the dead. No one was allowed out except on duty, and even then you were expected to go about singly and to hug the walls instead of walking in the middle of the pavement or the road. But after sunset the whole place would spring to life. The streets would be crowded and the shops would open up. The cheap jewellers in the *rue Gambetta* must have done a roaring trade selling trinkets to the troops. The theatre, too, would be open and here the various divisional concert parties would rival one another in giving 'all-star' performances to crowded houses.

Another strange feature of our stay in Arras that January was our situation in the line. The trenches we occupied were in the suburb of Blangy. A few houses were still standing and our company headquarters occupied one of them—a pleasant little villa with a bowl of goldfish in the drawing-room and a nude statue of Venus at the bottom of the garden (the statue was chipped about a bit as it served as a target for revolver practice). The trenches themselves were just across the road : good bricked-up trenches they were, running north to the banks of the river Scarpe : and your footsteps could easily be heard as you walked along them. So could those of the German sentries as they paced along *their* trenches, which in this small section of the line were no more than ten or fifteen yards away from ours. The closeness of the two lines was a good insurance against strafing on either side. The mildest exchange of hand grenades or bombs, still more of minenwerfers, would have made life quite intolerable.

But now we had come away from all that and were behind
the lines, training for what we all knew was going to be the
'spring offensive'. A stretch of country was chosen which more or
less resembled the ground we should have to attack over. Imagination, we were told, was necessary in order to fill in gaps in the
landscape and to remove one or two features that should not have
been there. For the rest, our job was to 'get used to' the lie of the
land ('getting to know the course', I called it in memory of golf-
ing days) and also to accustom ourselves to the new battle-forma-
tion, which involved advancing in little 'blobs' instead of in the
usual line.

A healthy life it was—up early in the morning: a route march
to the field of operations; a couple of hours advancing in 'blobs';
a break for lunch; a further advance in the afternoon, culminat-
ing, naturally enough, in the capture of our objective; the
Colonel's pow-wow on the day's achievement; the march back
with Dawson taking the salute as we entered the village to the
tune of 'A Hundred Pipers'; and so home to billets. After tea, a
foot inspection or possibly a kit inspection; and the evening spent
in writing or censoring letters or checking lists (in the Hodge
tradition), while a gramophone screeched the latest tunes from
the revues; or, as an occasional variation, dinner at the officers'
club in Avesnes-le-Compte. Sometimes on fine mornings Gilbert
and I would get up early and go riding. Then the war was forgotten. All we cared for was the brightness of the morning, the
sight of the girls, women and old men working in the fields, and
the joy of living and of being in each other's company.

III

Leave—that flew like the wind. Ten days of it. The familiar
Hampstead flat my parents lived in appeared in a new light: the
repository in a changing world of things that did not change.
The worn leather seat of my father's armchair—it had always
been worn and slightly shabby ever since I could remember—
was a reassuring sight: good that it had not been patched or
mended. The drawing-room, too—that oddly furnished apart-
ment with the saddle-bag chairs, my mother's Broadwood grand,

LIEUT.-COL. W. R. A. DAWSON, D.S.O.
6th Battalion, Royal West Kent Regiment.
On October 23rd, 1918 an enemy shell burst almost on top of him. It was one of the last shells ever fired at the battalion. He died of his wounds at the 20th General Hospital, Camiers, on December 3rd, 1918.

LIEUT. GILBERT TRENCHARD CARRÉ
6th Battalion, Royal West Kent Regiment.
He was killed in action at Lateau Wood, near Cambrai, on November 20th,
1917.

a light oak bookcase with glass doors, and old-fashioned sofa—and its only-used-on-Sundays atmosphere. I looked over the familiar shelves and was comforted to see the books I knew so well. What an affection I had for their backs! Gilbart's *History of Banking* in two volumes (I had never opened it, but home would not have seemed like home without it), Hallam's *Middle Ages* in three volumes, Prescott's *Conquest of Peru, British Commerce 1763–1878* by Leone Levi, and overtopping them all, the ninth edition of the *Encyclopaedia Britannica*.

Never before, not even in my schooldays, had our pieces of Victorian furniture, our space-filling pictures and our china ornaments seemed so precious as they did on my first leave from France. They had an importance of their own—the importance of being familiar. They still form the principal part of the picture in my mind whenever I think of our 'drawing-room'.

Theatres (sometimes two a day), concerts, meals in restaurants, breakfast in bed, visits from elderly family friends (like old Miss Brooks, who had knitted me a pair of mittens because she had heard that you couldn't pull the trigger of a rifle properly if you were wearing gloves and she thought that mittens, while keeping my wrists warm, would leave my fingers free; or the two Miss Macfees who lived in the flat below and who were permitted by my mother to ask me questions but were not allowed to do much talking themselves; and of course Miss Lawford and Miss Schafer, retired schoolmistresses, who lived in the top flat in the block, and had, it seemed, read my letters home and practically committed them to memory)—everything was done by my parents to entertain me and to make me comfortable. Even Dorothy D——, always alluded to by my parents as 'a *very* nice girl', was invited to the flat to meet me. But Dorothy was tall, and tall girls frightened me: and she was rather dumb, almost as dumb as I was myself: she was also extremely refined, and the thought of enjoying any other relationship with her than that of sitting together at a tea-table and eating thin bread and butter was beyond imagination. Her visits, I think must have been as uncomfortable for her as they were for me.

Then the last day. No question of gadding about. My mother and I spent the time quietly pottering at home, pretending that the day had no particular significance. Apart from an occasional word from her ('You will write every day, won't you—even if it's only one of those printed postcards?') and an assurance from me that life at the Front was very different from what was generally imagined, that most of the time we spent in jollification behind the lines and that anyway the chances of being hit, worked out mathematically, were infinitesimal—apart from such little exchanges we kept off the war. More to the point were the things we were all going to do when the war was over—shaping themselves in my mind as vague but spacious plans for a GOOD TIME, and in the minds of my parents as a reversion to routine and normal life.

In the evening my father came home earlier than usual from his office.

'I've been thinking,' he announced in the voice of one on the brink of discovery, 'how would it be if I sent you out a body-shield?'

'A body-shield!' I exclaimed. 'Good heavens, what on earth for?'

'Why, to protect you...'

'A very good idea!' nodded my mother.

I became contemptuous.

'Really!' I said. 'What good do you think a body-shield would be? To begin with I shouldn't be able to move in it—'

'Why not?' asked my father.

'Because of its weight.'

'I'd get you a light one.'

'And in the second place,' I went on, 'they're perilous things, these body-shields. I knew a man who had one. He never recovered from it.'

'How d'you mean?'

'A bullet hit him and drove the metal of the body-shield into the wound. They're no good at all.'

We argued for some time about body-shields. But neither of us would concede a point. Then we gave it up and spent a subdued evening, trying to be as cheerful as we could.

At ten o'clock I said I supposed it was time to be getting a move on. My train went from Victoria very early next morning,

and so as to be sure of catching it I was to spend the night in a
hostel just outside the station—where the statue of Marshal Foch
now stands.

I took a last look round the flat and then we left, the three of
us, in a cab for Victoria. We didn't talk much on the journey.

Outside the hostel I said good-bye and then walked up the
pathway leading to the front door. Before going in I turned
and waved to them and shouted 'good night'. They were standing where I had left them. In answer to my shout my father
saluted.

IV

Now our period of training was over and we moved up into
Arras. But instead of occupying empty houses this time we were
billeted in cellars. Something (besides spring) was in the air and
we knew that the day of 'the push' was near. For us the sooner
it came the better. We had been preparing for it for two months
and it was (we had been told) going to be 'a really first-class
show'. To begin with a stupendous bombardment lasting ten
whole days! Think of it! (they said). The old Boche will be
knocked to a pulp. Ten days of the heaviest bombardment ever
known in the history of this or any other war! Real heavy stuff
too. Meanwhile our boys would be lying doggo—safe and away
from it all—so that whatever Fritz put over in reply simply
wouldn't touch us. We should be as safe as houses—or, consider-
ing the state of most of the houses in Arras, infinitely safer.

These cheering announcements we duly passed on to the men,
most of whom were (like some of us) young and inexperienced
enough to lap them up with glee. The war, it seemed, was going
to be a walkover.

But how exactly were we to be 'safe and away from it all'?
What did that mean?

We were soon to know.

One day, during the last week of March, we received our
orders. As every movement was to be shrouded in secrecy, we
did not even emerge from our cellars, lest the Germans might
see us from the air. Instead we crept along them, passing from
one to another, through holes knocked in the walls. Presently we

came to some steps down. At the bottom we found ourselves in a large circular tunnel. A gangway of boards ran along one side of this electrically-lit passage, while along the bottom flowed a stream of water. We were in fact in the main drain of Arras. The war was full of queer experiences: but we had never imagined that we should be going into battle down the drain.

For a mile or so we trudged along this drain, emerging at length, much as Aladdin emerged, into a vast cave; only here the light was reflected not by jewels but by chalk. The caves (for there was a series of them) were fitted with every modern convenience: electric light, running water, braziers for cooking, a miniature railway and even furniture, though this consisted mostly of empty crates and petrol cans.

Here, in these caves, we lived for over a week. No sound reached us from the outer world. Very occasionally a small chip of chalk would drop from the roof, sign that a heavy shell had landed overhead.

From time to time we climbed to one of the exits debouching into the reserve trenches and took the air. From this part of the line we had a good view of the German positions and also of the effects of our non-stop bombardment. As far as we could see to the north and to the south, the German trenches were being pounded out of recognition. Great towers of earth were being flung up all along the eastern skyline and the air was full of whirring iron. Not much was coming from the German side.

'They're saving it up till the show begins,' said Gilbert. We were standing in the reserve trenches, watching the barrage.

'What will you feel like,' I asked him, 'when the show begins?'

I think the question surprised him. The truth was that I didn't know how I was going to take this coming battle. I supposed that if others could go through with it, I could, too. But I was not sure.

'I think,' Gilbert answered, 'that if I thought about it, I should be terrified.'

'I can't help thinking about it.'

'You're braver than I am.'

'What nonsense!' I said, shortly. 'I'm terrified too—just as much as you'd be if you thought about it.'

'You manage not to show it.'

I shrugged my shoulders. 'It's being with other people,' I said. 'The feeling that you're all in the same boat together. If you weren't with me now, standing here, I should be afraid— more afraid than I am.'

Gilbert nodded.

'I feel the same when I'm with you,' he said. 'As a matter of fact I feel more afraid for you than I do for myself.'

I laughed and told him I would be all right. But I was moved by what he had said. I knew it was true.

'The people I'm sorry for,' I said, 'are the people at home. We all know what's happening to us. They don't. It's not knowing that's the devil.'

'I believe you like being out here, Alan.'

'No, I don't. I wish to God the whole thing was over. But while it's on I'd rather be here than anywhere else.'

'You wouldn't say that if you'd been through the Somme.'

'I don't suppose I should,' I admitted. 'I might not be saying it this time next week, when we've been through this show—if we do get through it.'

'I wish to God it was over,' said Gilbert, '—the whole thing, I mean.'

'But as long as it isn't?'

'As long as it isn't— we must be together.'

We stood gazing at the sunny landscape tortured by our guns. Now and then a shell from one of the German heavies slithered over, making a whirring noise above our heads, then fading away, to burst far behind our lines.

'Do you believe,' I asked, 'in survival after death?'

'No,' said Gilbert promptly. 'Do you?'

I did at the time, and said so.

'How do you picture it?' he asked.

'I don't know. But it'll be very grand...'

Gilbert smiled.

'Marble stairways and streets paved with gold?'

'Perhaps. I don't know. But what I can't imagine is the idea of being snuffed out like a candle. Everything can't end—just like that.'

'I can't imagine,' Gilbert replied, 'how it can end any other way. I wish I could. My father's a parson and believes in all these things. I can't.'

'Well,' I said, 'I suppose it's a matter of faith.'

To tell the truth I felt a little shocked. My religious teaching had been conventional. It had never occurred to me to question it. On the contrary I had rather taken to religion. Jimmy's Sunday morning talks had kindled feelings of devotion in me that expressed themselves in faith rather than in good works. I had had, it is true, a bad moment on discovering shortly before my confirmation that I had never been baptised. To have lived for nearly a decade and a half outside the state of grace would, I felt, want a good deal of excusing. My father's explanation was that he had preferred to leave the decision to me when I should reach a responsible age, rather than take it for me when I was a baby. There was common sense in this view, but I could not help wishing that he had taken a risk and acted as other parents had. Nor was I much reassured when I heard that the only godparents who could be scraped together for me at short notice were Roley and his wife (known as 'Mother Roley'). Time pressed and though from my point of view these two were a pretty poor substitute for the real thing, I had the impression from them that they were acting rather nobly—as though they were hushing up a scandal.

My baptism took place in the Parish Church, just in time for me to be confirmed. Ever since I had been faithful to the Church.

'But don't you believe in Jesus, then?' I put the question with some nervousness, fearing not that I should be shaken in my faith, but that he might be offended.

'I don't believe,' Gilbert replied, 'in all the stories that are told about Him. But I believe His way of life is the one to follow.'

'But the divinity of Jesus—don't you believe in that?'

'No. Anyway, that doesn't seem to me important.'

'He was just an ordinary man...?'

'Not ordinary. But He was a man—at least, if He ever existed. Meyrick says there's doubt about it.'

'Doubt about the existence of Jesus!' I exclaimed.

'So Meyrick says. He's frightfully clever. I hope you'll meet him one day, Alan. You'd like each other.'

'Well, *I'm* not frightfully clever,' I said. 'I s'pose that's why I've never heard this theory—I mean, about Jesus never having existed. Do you believe it?'

'I don't know. It sounds pretty incredible to me. But He may have been like Homer. There was no one person called Homer. He was a lot of people—a kind of tradition. It may have been the same with Jesus.'

'I can imagine all sorts of stories growing up round Jesus, sayings being attributed to Him and all that. But to say that He never existed—'

Gilbert smiled.

'I didn't know you felt so strongly about it,' he said.

'Well, you see—' I tried awkwardly to explain, '—I pray quite a lot. Don't you ever pray?'

'I used to. But I don't pray much now.'

'I pray a lot,' I said solemnly. 'I should feel...sort of lost if I didn't pray. I believe that...'

'What do you believe?'

I had paused because I was half afraid that Gilbert might laugh at me.

'I believe that no harm can come to you unless God intends that it shall.'

Gilbert didn't laugh.

'I wish I could believe that,' he said. 'But even if I did, I don't really see that it'd be any safeguard. There's no reason why God should want to protect anyone specially, is there? Anyway I'm sure He wouldn't want to protect *me*!'

'Well, He might,' I suggested feebly.

'Besides, if I prayed to Him to protect me and He didn't want to—what then? I don't see that my praying would affect His decision one way or the other.'

'You never know.'

'You mean it's as well to be on the safe side? Praying might help and anyway it can't do any harm?'

'I think I should put it more positively than that,' I said, conscious that I wasn't making out much of a case for prayer.

To my surprise Gilbert nodded.

'I think you're probably right,' he said.

For the first time in my life, I began to feel some doubt.

V

Zero hour was to have been on April 7th, but for some reason, known only to the brass hats, Z day became X day and the attack was put off for forty-eight hours. We wondered whether the postponement had anything to do with America's entry into the war, news of which had just reached us. But we never knew.

So on Easter Monday, April 9th, 1917, at one o'clock in the morning, we filed out of the great chalk caves of Arras and took up our positions in the trenches. After all the rehearsals we had been put through we knew exactly what to do. I had three officers with me in my company—Gilbert, Hibbert (the erstwhile shoe-maker corporal) and Marling Apperley. The last-named had been with us about two months. He was slightly my senior in years and set us all an example in conscientiousness and fixity of purpose. The trouble was he did talk rather a lot.

Our precise objective was a set of trenches some four miles ahead, on the outskirts of what once had been a village. The cluster of battered houses, grouped round the summit of a little hill, was visible for miles and had become a familiar sight to all of us ever since we had come to Arras. The name of the place was Monchy-le-Preux.

The attack was timed for 5.30, just as dawn was breaking. We were to await no signal, but as soon as the hands on our synchronised watches pointed to the half-hour we were to go forward.

At a quarter past five I took a last look round, seeing that my men were in position. The formation was familiar : we had practised it a score of times and each man knew exactly where his place was and what he had to do. At first we were to advance in little 'blobs'—ten men or so to each 'blob'. After that when I blew my whistle the 'blobs' were to open out into line. Thereafter the platoon commanders were to exercise discretion, directing the men to lie down and open fire or to advance, according to the situation. The men were all in excellent spirits and anxious, so far as I could judge, to get on with the show.

A few minutes before the half hour I returned to my own position in the middle of the company. My sergeant-major was waiting for me. He was standing with a little group of signallers and runners—my own particular 'blob'—and when I appeared he sprang smartly to attention, saluted and reported in peacetime parade fashion that all were 'present and correct'. The formality amused me and in a queer way gave me confidence.

I stood looking at my watch. Exactly at the half-hour the curtain of our barrage lifted and at the same moment along twenty-six miles of front, so far as the eye could see to the north and to the south, the sky was lit by the golden rain of German rockets signalling the S.O.S. Twenty-six miles of golden rain! The show could hardly have had a more spectacular beginning.

We moved forward. We did not run. We walked. What before had appeared as a deserted landscape now became a crowded battlefield. Everywhere men were moving forward. Guns roared. Aeroplanes swooped. Machine-guns rattled. In the pandemonium it was impossible to hear one's own voice, still less anybody else's. I looked at my seregant-major and nodded. He grinned back at me. I wondered how, in all this din my whistle would be heard when the time came for me to blow it. At present the company was holding its general formation. But the ground was rough and pitted with shell-holes, and as the men scrambled in and out of them some of the 'blobs' were beginning to straggle.

We passed over no-man's land, thick with broken wire, and into the enemy's lines. The trenches, as we expected, were deserted. Instead of meeting Germans, we were greeted with their gunfire. Black high explosive shells burst overhead with that cracking, wrenching noise that blew the breath out of your body. But they did small damage. Now and then a piece of metal hurtled by with a zip and buried itself in the earth. Sometimes spent machine-gun bullets came moaning through the air. For the rest we moved forward without hindrance. The advance was beginning to look like a walk-over.

Suddenly, two or three hundred yards away to the right, a heavy shell landed among the advancing troops. For the first time in my life I saw human bodies and limbs hurled into the air. I swallowed, trying hard not to feel afraid. The sergeant-major glanced round at me. I nodded to him as cheerily as I knew how.

'Fun's just beginning!' I shouted.

I doubt if he heard me. But he smiled. The sight of a man smiling reassured me.

We continued to move forward. The high-explosive 'crumps' were less frequent now, but the heavy shells were still falling and the machine-guns were becoming more insistent. So far we had seen no sign of the enemy. As for our 'blobs', they were hardly recognisable. They had in fact opened out of their own accord. Since we were now making our way over a system of deep trenches it was impossible for the men to keep to any fixed formation. Parties of them were advancing along communication trenches. Others were running forward over the top.

Crossing a trench I glanced down and saw one of our men lying in a pool of blood. His body had been split from the shoulder, downwards, and some of his entrails were hanging out. I paused, not because I wanted to look, but because I could not turn away. I had seen a dead body before, but never one so mutilated. I did not feel physically sick. I felt frightened and shaky. My knees nearly gave way under me.

With an effort I pulled myself together and hurried on. But the image of what I had seen remained with me for hours afterwards. So long as I live I shall never be able to obliterate it altogether.

Now our men, taking advantage of such cover as there was, were going forward more or less at random. Mingled with them were men of the flanking battalions, and they were taking orders, all of them, from any officers that were about. In the distance I saw for the first time the grey uniforms of the Germans. The men were running back as hard as they could go. But nearer to us—about two hundred yards ahead— a machine-gun was rattling away, covering the retirement with a sweeping fire. I joined a line of our men who were firing at this gun. (They were 'our' men, though not men of my battalion.) They lay flat—flatter, I thought, than they would have done on a rifle range—but their fire was reaching its mark. In a few minutes the machine-gun ceased firing. The moment had come for us to advance. I got up and blew my whistle signalling to the men to go forward. At the same moment I felt a smarting pain in my thigh and found myself lying on the ground. My hand, when I drew it away from the place on my thigh, was covered with blood.

'Are you badly hurt, sir?' a voice asked.

'I don't think so,' I said, gingerly feeling the place again. I had no idea how I had been wounded or how badly.

'You stay here, sir,' the voice said. 'I'll get the stretcher bearers.'

'No,' I said, conscious of seeming heroic. 'I'll be all right.'

The truth was that, after feeling the place and pressing gently on the bone and then moving my leg, I was beginning to wonder whether I had been wounded at all. Had it not been for the blood I should have said that nothing more deadly than a pea-shooter had found its mark.

Even the blood had congealed.

Turning on my side, I saw that the men I had signalled to had gone forward and had reached the trench where the machine-gun had been lodged. As I watched them I felt less and less of a hero and more and more of a fraud.

Presently I got up, the owner of the voice giving me a hand.

'Are you feeling better, sir?' enquired the unknown soldier. His solicitude would have sounded well if I had been seriously wounded.

'I'm all right,' I snapped. 'There's nothing the matter with me at all.'

'It was a narrow shave, sir. I thought that there sniper had got yer that time. Would you like me to go back with yer, sir?'

At this I lost my temper. I couldn't help it. My 'wound', which was no more than a scratch, had made me smart. It had also made me feel a fool. And here was this chap (whose help, God knows, I should have been glad enough to have, had I been badly hit) offering to escort me back. I cursed him and even accused him of wanting to go back himself.

'I don't want to go back, sir,' he mumbled. 'I was only—'

'Come on, then!' I shouted.

We reached the trench which was one of the main lines of the

German defence system and jumped down into it. At the entrance to one of the deep dugouts two of our men were standing with their rifles cocked while a stream of Germans filed out, each man holding his hands above his head. Their field grey uniforms almost matched the colour of their faces. Pale, lustreless and fearful, they lined up at the order of a British sergeant and looked as if they had had enough of it all.

Leaving these prisoners I made my way along the trench in search of my own men. I was alone now and though I could hear plenty of firing and explosions in the distance the place immediately round me was quiet. It was as if the battle had passed over like a storm and disappeared. I thought of the scheme we had so carefully rehearsed. I thought (with a sinking heart) of the Colonel. Also of Hibbert and Marling Apperley. Above all of Gilbert. What had happened to them?

I had gone about fifty yards when I heard the sound of a rifle being fired. Rounding the bend of the trench I came upon the man who had fired it.

'It's that bugger there,' he remarked as he saw me, 'not twenty yards away. I'll get him yet!'

Those were the last words that soldier spoke. As he turned to fire again the air was split by the crack of a bullet and he fell—hit clean through the forehead.

'It's an unhealthy spot you're going to, sir,' remarked a voice behind me. I turned to face the man who had helped me up. 'I saw you coming up this way and thought I'd follow,' he added apologetically.

I felt I had wronged this man. But I did not know what he was doing hanging round—any more than I knew what I myself was doing.

'You're from the Buffs,' I said. 'Where's your battalion?'

'I don't know, sir,' he replied. 'I reckon I've lost 'em.'

I could scarcely blame him, seeing that I had lost the company I myself was supposed to be commanding.

'I'd like if you don't mind, sir,' he added, 'to have a go at that there Jerry.'

'We'll both have a go at him,' I said, picking up the dead man's rifle. So we would have done, if we had been able to spot the place where the sniper was hiding. But though we clambered out of the trench (incidentally offering him a momentary target) he gave no sign. We slithered along from shell-hole to shell-hole in the direction of his shot. We never found him.

'Reckon he's done a bunk,' observed my companion.

If he had, his last shot had gone home.

Then in the trench below I saw Gilbert.

VI

Gilbert was making his way in our direction. He was followed by half a dozen of his men.

I hailed him with a shout of joy. He and his men were surprised (they even showed signs of being pleased) to see me.

'We didn't know where you were,' Gilbert exclaimed. 'We thought you'd been hit—like poor old Apperley.'

'Apperley?'

'Badly, I'm afraid. They've taken him down.'

'And Hibbert?'

'Hibbert's all right. He's consolidating, about a quarter of a mile away. It's all clear now, so far as we've come. I was just going to make contact with the Buffs.'

'There was a sniper—' I began.

'We got him,' said Gilbert. 'Harris and Shoesmith laid him out between them.'

'And a good job, too,' observed the man from the Buffs, who was standing by my side.

'Where's the rest of the company?' I asked, putting the best face I could on my ignorance.

'They're in position all right,' replied Gilbert. 'And the others have gone through.'

By 'the others' he meant the Brigade that had been coming up behind us to continue the advance after we had gained our objectives. In other words, so far as we were concerned, the battle was over and we had done all that had been expected of us!

'Well,' I said, with feelings of mingled relief and astonishment, 'that's fine!'

I had an uncomfortable feeling that my part in the battle had been precisely nil. It appeared to me that I had reached our objective 'by another route'. However, there I was and there was Gilbert. The relief at seeing him was very great.

That night we spent consolidating our position in the newly-captured trenches. Our long-range guns were still firing and all round us there was great activity. Battalions of troops were pouring ahead and supplies were being brought up from the rear. I ordered the men to work in relays, and of the three officers I arranged that two should always be on duty. But I doubt if anyone got any sleep: for on top of all the noise and excitement the weather had sharpened. Earlier in the day sleet had been falling. By the evening the sleet had turned to snow. All night snow fell. In the morning a thick mantle lay upon the ground.

During the whole of the next day the vast activity continued. Men, guns, lorries, mules, cyclists, staff cars, and all the paraphernalia of an army on the move filled in the scene for miles and miles around us. Rumours flew from mouth to mouth. There was talk of a break-through, and when the cavalry came up, passing within a few hundred yards of us, on their way to Monchy, we really believed that a gap in the line had been made and that the enemy's flank was about to be turned. As the horsemen passed us we cheered them on their way.

That evening orders came for us to move forward again. When darkness fell, guides led us through the snow. The men were tired but in good heart, exhilarated not only by the feel of victory but also by the experience of movement and open warfare after the monotonous immobility of trench life. Anything, they said, to get a move on.

After trudging a mile or so over difficult, broken ground in the dark, we were halted and told to dig ourselves in. Ahead some sort of artillery strafe appeared to be going on. But the shells were not falling near us and we didn't worry. A staff officer gave us a line, running roughly from north to south, and said that that was the position we were to defend in case of counter-attack. The word, I remember, took us by surprise. We knew that after you had made an attack, a counter-attack might be expected. But the push we had been in was more than an attack. It was

an 'offensive'. To counter it the old Boche would have to stage
an offensive of his own—if indeed he could stage anything at all,
which we doubted. Anyway if there had been a 'breakthrough',
why worry about a counter-attack? However, we had been
ordered to dig, and as the night was cold we set to with a will.
Under the snow we found the remains of battle—equipment,
rifles, hand grenades and, here and there, dead bodies. (One body
was that of a Scotsman in a kilt. I have the impression he had
been frozen to death.) We also found some German field rations
—tinned stuff which wasn't to our taste.

Then—when we had been digging for an hour—we were told
to move on again. I asked the staff officer who gave us the order
if he was quite sure that he had got hold of the right company,
as only an hour before we had been told to dig in where we were.
All he said was that there was a war on and that we ought to be
dam' glad we were advancing.

So we pulled ourselves together and moved on.

By now the dawn was taking the edge off the darkness and
when we reached our new position we saw that we were but a
few hundred yards north of the ruins of Monchy—which meant
that since the morning of the ninth we had advanced five miles.
Five miles in those days was an unheard-of distance for an infantry advance. At the same time we were told that this new position was in full view of the enemy and that we had better dig
like hell for the next half hour, because as soon as day broke
we should have to lie doggo. 'Diggin' our graves, I calls it,' observed one lad in my company as he struck the ground with his
entrenching tool.

I did what I could to encourage the men—mainly by setting
to myself as hard as I knew how—and by the time the half hour
was up a trench had been dug just deep enough to give us cover.
For the whole of the day we lay in this improvised trench, the
sentries keeping watch by means of periscopes. It was impossible
to see the Boche, but we were told that he was occupying the
slope opposite. And we believed it, for his snipers were busy and
we dared not show our heads above ground. That day was one of
the longest I remember.

When night came we dug again. But the men, for all that they had spent an idle day, were tired and spiritless. The cold, I think, had got them under—and the realisation that after all the end of the war was not 'just round the corner'. Of hot food there was none. We lived on our iron rations and such extras as we could scrounge, mostly from the haversacks of the dead. For Gilbert and me one of the servants had 'found' half a bottle of whisky. Though we welcomed the find we also felt a trifle ashamed of taking it. But what could we do? There were at least a hundred and fifty men with us. What was half a bottle among so many?

'We could throw it away,' suggested Gilbert, reducing the problem to an absurdity.

'Or we could give it to the sergeant-major,' I said.

'Which would come to the same thing,' retorted Gilbert.

So we comforted ourselves not only with the whisky but also with the reflection that in taking care of ourselves we were acting in the best interests of the company. For now we were the only two officers left, Marling Apperley having been wounded and Hibbert having gone down sick the day before. We could not have been much to look at, the two of us, huddled there in our cubby-hole, with three days' growth on our chins. Nor were the conditions very grand. We were tired and cold and we knew that at any moment the Boche might start bombarding us. Yet, being together, I do not think we were unhappy.

As dusk was falling on the evening of the second day we saw a runner coming towards us from the direction of Monchy. We watched him, wondering what his news was. We hoped he would tell us we were going to be relieved.

'The Colonel's compliments, sir,' announced the messenger, 'and 'e would like to see you at seven o'clock at 'is 'eadquarters.'

'What's the news?' I asked.

'Dunno wot the news is, sir,' replied the other, 'but I reckon as our cavalry boys 'ave copped it up at Monchy.'

'How do you mean?'

'Reckon you'll see wot I mean, sir, when you goes up there.'

With a quarter of an hour in hand I left Gilbert in charge of the company and started off for Monchy, the runner showing me the way.

'For God's sake get us relieved,' Gilbert said, as I departed. 'The men are all in.'

I said I would do what I could.

In five minutes we were at the foot of the village. As we turned the bend of the road to go up the hill, I stopped. The sight that greeted me was so horrible that I almost lost my head. Heaped on top of one another and blocking up the roadway for as far as one could see lay the mutilated bodies of our men and their horses. These bodies, torn and gaping, had stiffened into fantastic attitudes. All the hollows of the road were filled with blood.

This was the cavalry.

As I learnt afterwards, when our horsemen had gathered in Monchy the German had put down a box barrage round the place—the four sides of the barrage gradually drawing inwards. The result of this shooting lay before me. Nothing that I had seen before in the way of horrors could be even faintly compared with what I saw around me now. Death in every imaginable shape was there for the examining.

I walked up the hill, picking my way as best I could and often slipping in the pools of blood, so that my boots and the lower parts of my puttees were dripping with blood by the time I reached the top. Nor, I discovered on my way up, were all the men and animals quite dead. Now and then a groan would strike the air—the groan of a man who was praying for release. Sometimes the twitch of a horse's leg would shift the pattern of the heaped-up bodies. A small party of stretcher-bearers, obviously unequal to their task, were doing what they could to relieve the suffering.

I found the Colonel in the cellar. He was now in charge not only of the battalion and of the whole brigade, but also of the situation generally. He had, characteristically enough, assumed command of it on his own initiative, and when I arrived he was telling a battery commander where and when he was to fire his guns. It was a gloomy place, this cellar. It was lit by two candles and smelt of death. The only cheerful sight in it reposed on a table in a corner—an enormous ham. It was the only thing that any of us felt like attacking.

When the other three company commanders had arrived,

Dawson spoke to us. He said that things had not gone exactly according to plan. The cavalry, instead of staging a break-through, had been trapped—as any fool could have told they would be, except apparently our Higher Command. The result was that the whole show had come more or less to a standstill. That was a situation—and it had to be remedied at once. Every hour would make a difference, because it would give the Boche that much more time to dig in and rally his strength for a counter-attack. Our orders therefore were to press on as rapidly as possible at all costs. This meant staging an attack at dawn.

Dawson paused. Perhaps he was waiting for one of us to say something. We knew better than to open our mouths before our opinion was invited.

'Well,' he said presently, 'have you got anything to say? You, Porteous?'

Porteous commanded A company.

'Well, sir, if we have to attack, we'll attack. But we shan't put up much of a show, I'm afraid. The men haven't got it in them. They're cold and they're hungry and they haven't slept for four nights. They ought to be relieved. But they'll do what they're ordered.'

Dawson grunted. Turning to me, he asked me what I thought.

'I say the same, sir,' I replied. I told him that my men were exhausted and that if an attack was to be made fresh troops ought to be used. But I said, as Porteous had said, that we would of course do what we were ordered.

The other two company commanders said the same.

'It's all very well,' observed Dawson, 'to talk about fresh troops. But they've got to be up here in time to go over the top at half past five in the morning. It's now past seven.'

'Couldn't the show be put off,' suggested Porteous, 'for twenty-four hours?'

'If you'd listened to what I said," retorted Dawson, 'you'd know why that's impossible.'

'Would you like to come and see my men for yourself, sir?' Porteous enquired.

'If I had time to go round the battalion, d'you think I'd be

sitting in this blasted cellar!' retorted Dawson. 'If there was anyone here at all who had the remotest idea of how to take charge
or to do anything except tell me that all his men are exhausted—'

'I'm telling you the truth, sir!' interrupted Porteous, with a
temerity we all admired.

For a second I thought Dawson was going to lose his temper.
But he realised in time, as we all realised, that Porteous was talking sense.

'I know you are,' said Dawson quietly. 'And you're quite right.
In ordinary circumstances I'd tell the Division to put the show
off for twenty-four hours so as to give the men a chance—or else
send new men in. But these circumstances aren't ordinary. For
the last four days we've had the Boche on the run as we've never
had him on the run before. I believe that even now it's not too
late to keep him on the run, if we follow up at once. Remember
he's checked us already. The cavalry who were supposed to go
through are—well, you can see for yourselves where they are.
Now that he's checked us the first thing he'll do will be to counter
attack—if we give him the time. As things are even twenty-four
hours will make a difference. That's why, if we're going to make
a success of this push, we've got to go on first thing in the morning. And don't forget this. We were the leading brigade to go
over on the ninth. We saw some fighting: but it wasn't so fierce
and we didn't meet the resistance which some of the other
brigades met—the brigades that leap-frogged us. They were up
against it more than we were: and their casualties were heavier
than ours. Now we've leap-frogged them and it's our turn again.
I don't propose to tell the Division that we can't go on.'

He paused and looked at us. He was sitting on a backless chair
behind an upturned crate which was used for a table. The light
from the candles cast upward shadows on his face. Behind him
stood the adjutant, whose expression showed clearly that he sym-
pathised with us and at the same time shared the Colonel's views.
His gaze was accordingly directed to the floor.

'I want you therefore,' continued Dawson presently, 'to warn
your men. They'd better get all the rest they can tonight—don't
put them on digging parties or anything of that sort. They must

be ready to go over at 5.30 in the morning—as soon as the order comes from me.'

'We don't go over till we get your order?' one of us asked.

'You don't go over till you get the order from me,' repeated Dawson. 'But you must be ready. Do you understand?'

We all four said we understood.

After waiting about half-a-minute, Dawson said:

'If that's clear, there's one thing I'll add. I've been trying all the afternoon, and I'm still trying, to arrange a relief tonight—'

'A relief tonight!' one of us interrupted. 'D'you mean, sir—?'

'Don't I make myself clear?' demanded Dawson sternly. 'I tell you that I'm trying, and have been trying all the afternoon, to arrange for the battalion to be relieved—tonight. So far, I haven't had definite word. I've told the Division what I know myself of the state the men are in: and I shall tell them now what you've told me this evening. But if they can't arrange it, then we shall attack. I expect to have definite news before midnight. If the relief is coming, the code word will be 'orange'. If the relief is not coming and we have to go over the code word will be 'green'. I'll let you have word as soon as I can. That's all.'

The Colonel rose, indicating that the conference was over.

'Bring some whisky,' he ordered, 'and half-a-dozen mugs.' And then, turning to us, he said, 'There's just time for a drink. But I shouldn't advise you to linger on the way back. They've a habit of shelling this place about this time of the evening and you're better at a distance.'

He then asked me how I was off for food. I told him we were on iron rations and anything else we could get. He said that rations would be coming up about nine o'clock that evening and that a rum ration would also be included, which he advised us to hold till the morning.

We drank our whisky, saluted the Colonel and departed. I wondered whether we should ever meet again. If we didn't, my last memory of Dawson would be of a man secure in his authority, one whose stature was heightened by adversity. I understood how it was that men would follow him to hell.

In the gathering gloom I picked my way down the hill, stumbling against the bodies of horses and men. As I reached the bottom a shell whined over from the east and burst fifty yards behind us—uncomfortably near.

'The evening strafe,' observed the runner who was with me.

As he spoke, another shell came over, and then another and another.

'How long,' I asked, 'does the evening strafe last?'

'They keeps it up for about 'alf an hour'.

The shells were falling farther up the hill now—round about the place we had just left.

We hurried on.

Gilbert was relieved to see me. He had heard the shelling in Monchy and had been anxious.

When I told him of the interview his only comment was that oranges were his favourite fruit.

The next thing was to tell the sergeant-major. If on previous occasions I had thought him a man of no imagination, for that reason I looked more kindly on him now.

'I've just been seeing the Colonel,' I said. 'We must be ready to go over in the morning.'

'Go over in the morning, sir,' he repeated with emotionless precision. 'Very good, sir.'

'At 5.30.'

'At 5.30. Very good, sir. I'll warn the men.'

'But we don't go over, until we get the word.'

Then I asked:

'How d'you think the men'll feel about it, sergeant-major?'

He gave me the look of one who had been asked an irrelevant riddle.

'Feel about it, sir?'

'They seem a bit exhausted to me,' I suggested.

'They've been resting all day, sir,' retorted the sergeant-major, who was an old regular and had his own ideas about some of the new drafts. 'If they're going over in the morning they can go on resting most of the night.'

'Of course they can,' I said. 'Let them rest as long as possible.'

'Very good, sir.'

The question, so far as he was concerned, was closed—if indeed it had ever been open—and I knew there was no point in pressing him. It may be now that with all the changes in the Army the old type of sergeant-major has completely disappeared, and his place been taken by an educated and imaginative species —an obvious improvement. Yet the stolid, unquestioning obedience of such men as Sergeant-major Harris was not without its virtue. You could at least depend on him to stand fast : and the tighter the corner, the faster he would stand—even when it might have been more prudent to retire, a word of which Sergeant-major Harris did not know the meaning.

'There'll be a rum ration coming up later,' I said. 'We'd better keep it till ten minutes before zero.'

'Very good, sir.'

He was preparing to salute, when I handed out my little surprise.

'By the way,' I added casually, 'it's just possible that instead of going over in the morning we may be relieved tonight.'

If he felt surprise he did not show it. All he said was : 'May be relieved tonight, sir. Very good, sir.'

I made my last attempt to raise a smile.

'If we are to be relieved, I'll let you know!'

But it was no good. I might have been talking, as they say, to an automaton. I told him not to pass on anything to the men about a possible relief, in case they should be disappointed. And with his inevitable 'Very good, sir,' he departed.

After that I made a tour of the company. It was a dreary business. The men were huddled together in varying stages of exhaustion. A few were asleep : these were the luckier ones, unconscious of the cold and the discomfort. Here and there I was greeted with attempted cheeriness : 'Wot price a kip in the ole barn now, sir !' 'Reckon Jerry's got to Germany by now, I don't think !' 'Wish the General could see us now, sir !' But the majority endured in silence.

Returning to Gilbert I said that I wouldn't give much for our chances if we had to attack. Naturally we cursed the staff and wondered if they had the least idea how the show was going. We decided they hadn't. Regarding ourselves as the victims of incompetence we immediately began to feel superior. This was just as well, because whatever the truth may have been, unless we had been able to loose off our feelings on someone (and on whom better than the absent who are always wrong?), I think we might have found it difficult to carry on. As it was, we cheered up a lot and gave the ration party (who turned up about ten o'clock) a more hilarious welcome than they were expecting. The guide, it seemed, had lost his way and the Quartermaster Sergeant, a gloomy, conscientious man, had almost given up hope of reaching us at all.

In addition to the rations and the rum, he had brought up a few letters, among them one for me from my mother. Like most people, I have always enjoyed receiving letters (the joy of answering them has never been so great) and in those days the pleasure was acute—sharpened by the contrast which I invariably drew between the familiarity of the handwriting and of the Hampstead post-mark and the outlandishness of my surroundings when the letter was delivered. Every letter that I got from my mother or father (and I got one pretty nearly every day) recreated for me the surroundings of my home—the desk at which the letter was written, the brass inkstand and the blotter and even the particular brown-handled pen with its 'J' nib which my mother always used. I knew the pillar box at which the letter would have been posted : it stood just down the road, opposite the station. And here in France the letter was delivered to me a few days later in conditions which neither my father nor mother could picture—sometimes in a little farmhouse, sometimes under canvas, sometimes in a quiet sector of the trenches, sometimes in the front line. The last letter had come to me when we were in the great chalk caves in front of Arras. Now here was this one brought to me on the outskirts of Monchy, carried almost literally over the dead bodies of my comrades. There was the familiar writing. There the well-known Hampstead post-mark. Hampstead of all places! I was glad my mother did not know where I was when her letter was delivered. She would have died of fright. As it was I gave the Quartermaster Sergeant a field post-card to take back. Later, when we were back in billets, I would send a description of what we had been doing.

Now the rations had been taken over and the Quartermaster

Sergeant was preparing to depart. Had he, I asked discreetly, heard talk of a relief?

'A relief, sir? Can't say I have,' he answered. 'But there's a deal of to-ing and fro-ing at the back there. It's a job to know what's going on.'

We bade him good-night.

'See you tomorrow,' I said, 'though I don't know where you'll find us.'

'I hear you're going over in the morning,' he said.

'That's the idea.'

The Quartermaster Sergeant cleared his throat.

'The cavalry's had a bit of a chewing-up,' he observed.

'Well, we're not the cavalry,' I said, 'we're only the P.B.I. And we don't propose to get chewed up. If there's any chewing up to be done, we'll do it.'

'That's right, sir,' muttered the Quartermaster Sergeant doubtfully.

'And we shall have gone so far ahead,' I added, 'that you'll have a job to find us.'

'I shall find you all right, sir—if it takes me all night.'

'Well, I hope you will,' I said, knowing beyond a doubt that he would.

When he had gone, Gilbert asked me why I had spoken the way I had. I told him that the man had annoyed me by talking of the cavalry like that. Whereupon Gilbert reminded me that it was I who was always saying that it was better to take the gloomy view and then one wouldn't be disappointed.

'Well,' I said, 'there are times when it's up to someone to take a cheery view—even if I *do* think we're going to be chewed up like the cavalry!'

'*We* shan't be chewed up like the cavalry,' Gilbert said enthusiastically.

'I'm glad you don't think so.'

'Of course I don't,' he said. 'We shall be mown down like grass.'

Which was as good a joke as any other at that moment.

So far we had received no instructions. If we were to attack I had no idea what our objective was to be. Nor, I suspected, had anyone else, though Dawson had promised details of the plan. Even so there couldn't be much time to study them or pass them on to the company. The only thing to tell them, Gilbert suggested, was to advance and when they met the enemy defeat him. And that, I imagine, was what it would have come to—so far as instructions were concerned.

By eleven o'clock I had made up my mind that the chances of relief were nil. All I was concerned about was that we should get definite instructions as soon as posisble. I knew Dawson's difficulties and the time it took to get things moving. But I knew, too, how easily mistakes were made. Even in familiar surroundings you often lost your way, as I had known to my cost. Here the surroundings were wholly unfamiliar and it was dark. Easy enough for Dawson's runner to lose himself on the way from Monchy—and then where should we be? Perhaps even now he was wandering about with plans for the attack! I wondered what we ought to do if the instructions didn't come. Stand fast? Or attack? Gilbert said if he had his way a third of the company would attack, a third stand fast, and a third relieve themselves.

The minutes dragged slowly on and at half past eleven we were still without instructions. By that time a new problem had arisen. There was still a quarter of a bottle of whisky left. Should we drink it now? Should we drink it in the morning? Or should we drink none of it and take the bottle with us? If so, who should carry it? I was for taking it with us on the grounds that our plight might well become worse than it was now and then we should be glad we hadn't drunk it. Gilbert disagreed. He was for drinking it straight away on the grounds that we might as well make sure of it and that as for the morning—if we ever lived to see it—we still had our rum. The idea of taking the bottle with us was absurd, if only because we might get separated and he was certain to be the unlucky one. While we were still debating the question it began to snow. Gilbert said that was a sign from Heaven. If it was not a sign it was at least an encouragement. So between us we finished the bottle.

Just as we had finished it, I heard a challenge and a moment later Dawson's runner stood before me. Taking off his tin-hat he drew a scrap of paper from the lining and handed it to me. The message contained one word—'Orange'.

Twenty minutes later, just about midnight, the advance party of the relief arrived. They came from a battalion of the Essex regiment. The officer to whom I was to hand over had travelled far and was bewildered. I told him the length of line we were holding, the disposition of the different platoons, the location of our little store of ammunition and the direction of battalion headquarters.

'I know,' he said, 'roughly where battalion headquarters is, because I've just come from there. But which is the direction of the Boche?'

His question surprised me. I replied that so far as I knew the Boche was 'over there'. I pointed east. But if he thought otherwise...

The officer chuckled.

'I don't doubt it, if you say so,' he replied. 'But I've lost my direction and I thought I might as well know, that's all.'

In another half hour the main body of the relief came up. As soon as they had taken over, I sent Gilbert back with our men, remaining behind myself to show the Essex captain round the sector. That unilluminating process took me about half an hour. I then wished him luck and with the orderly I had kept with me, I started back.

We had five miles to go. It was dark at first and our pace was slow, the way being strewn with every kind of obstacle—deep shell-holes filled with slush, great masses of barbed wire, dead bodies of horses and of men, trench systems dotted with concrete pill-boxes and areas which had once been woods or copses and were now marked only with the broken stumps of trees. We made our way as best we could to the Arras–Cambrai road, and by the time we reached it the sun had risen, lighting up the white stones of the battered city. Whatever we may have felt about the war, most of us had an affection for Arras. There was a friendly atmosphere about the place, about its winding streets with their unexpected turns and alley ways, its magnificent squares, the *Grande Place* and the *Petite Place* with their colonnades and ornate house fronts, its ornamental park near the Baudimont

Gate and its little pleasure gardens where in peace-time the children used to play. In January, when we had first come to Arras, the German lines had run through the suburb of St. Sauveur on the eastern outskirts of the city: the Boche was literally down the street. Now, blasted out of his positions, he had gone. As we looked back on the mutilated buildings and the shell-scarred walls, I do not think that our affection for the city was diminished.

On reaching the road we took off our equipment and sat down to rest. We were tired. We had four days' growth on our faces and our clothes were plastered with mud. Our appearance, unthought of by ourselves, nevertheless attracted the attention of some passers-by. A friendly major, turning up from nowhere, extended an enormous silver flask towards us as we lay upon the ground.

'Get outside some of this,' he said. 'It'll do you good.'

We did as he told us. We each of us got outside a cupful of neat brandy. It did do us good.

The men in the caves were asleep when we got in. Picking my way over their bodies I came to my own place and lying down I slept for fifteen hours.

A few days later we heard that the Essex battalion which had relieved us up by Monchy had been counter-attacked at dawn and that of the whole battalion only eight came back—eight men in all.

VII

That then was the show—the great spring push—which some of us thought would be the beginning of the end. A push it had been, and a good-sized push at that. An advance of five miles on a twenty-mile front could fairly be counted as a major movement. But, as we soon learnt, it was not the beginning of the end. Our men had to clear out of Monchy and after about a month of fighting our line stabilised itself rather less than five miles east of Arras and remained in that position till the end.

Were we disappointed? I have no doubt that the more elderly among us were. As for the younger men, we soon forgot our disappointment in the pleasure of those three weeks rest that was granted to us. In war one learns to live from day to day. My own disappointment was further submerged by the fact that I was made a captain—promotion due to a minor wound which had sent the captain of D Company home. My only regret was that in leaving B Company I was also leaving Gilbert. But as things turned out the change made little difference to the time we were able to spend in one another's company. For in the next 'show' (it was the word we always used for any encounter with the Boche, from a raid to a large-scale offensive)—in the next show the battalion was in, on May 3rd, both Gilbert and I were ordered to remain behind, and as our losses on that occasion were far heavier than they had been in the push of April 9th I do not doubt that if Gilbert had gone in he would not have come back.

Being left out of a show meant that my feelings were mixed. This is what I wrote to my mother about it in a letter dated April 30th, 1917 :

I have just returned from seeing the battalion off into action. They passed through an old cemetery at 9.15. The brass band of the 7th Battalion (who are quite near here) stood at the side playing the Regimental March ('A Hundred Pipers') as the companies marched past at 200 yards distance. It was a glorious night and the moon lit up everything. I stood at the side of the track. My company was in the rear of the battalion, and I wished them all 'good luck' as they went past. Some of them said 'Cheeroh, sir'. There were about eight of us being left behind. It would be hard to describe our feelings. One realises the necessity for someone stopping behind and yet one can't settle down to it. We know that they are up there and yet we don't know what is happening. Some of our friends may be falling. I am glad to say the fellow I have spoken about to you before—by name Carré—. . . is also being left out.

As it was, we, too, had our share of excitement. The party left behind, officers, N.C.O.s and men, numbering, I suppose, about thirty in all, were billeted in a large house in the western quarter of Arras. On the evening of the 3rd, just after dinner, I had gone down the road to the Casualty Clearing Station in search of news. The C.C.S. would usually have the first news of any show in the sector. I had been away, I suppose, for about twenty minutes. When I came back I found that our house was on fire. The top storeys were well ablaze and as the only fire-extinguishing apparatus on the scene was a small French hand-pump which was worked by two people taking alternate pulls at the lever and threw up a jet like a soda-water syphon, it was only a matter of time before the whole building would be destroyed— as indeed it was. An incendiary shell had fallen on the house and killed a number of soldiers (signalmen and sergeant-majors' servants) who were sleeping in the attics.

I made my way through the crowd who were watching the fire and found my friend Stigand in charge of operations. This didn't surprise me, for Stigand was the sort of man who would naturally take charge in an emergency. He was an officer of long standing, wearing the South African ribbon, and should have been a colonel. As it was he was a lieutenant.

'There's one more case!' he was shouting when I reached him. I offered to go in and look for this last remaining case, who- ever he might be, and fetch him out. But Stigand was already in the doorway, hailing someone else who was on the stairs.

'It's all right,' Stigand shouted back at me. 'He's got it! That's the lot!'

Whereupon the mess corporal appeared carrying 'the case'— which was not, as I had supposed, a stretcher case, but a case of sherry. After Stigand had seen to it that everyone was safe (except only the poor fellows in the attics who, I gathered, had met with an instantaneous death) he had then, in the exercise of a powerful judgment, turned to the rescue of 'the cellar'. Under his supervision, reinforced by a display of personal courage on his part that was, I believe, a source of inspiration to all who served under him, every case, every bottle, even those already in use, were saved. It was an exploit of which he was, I think, justifi- ably proud.

But while our house had been hit by a stray shell, our battalion had been hit by something more deliberate—a devastating con- centration of rifle and machine-gun fire. From what I heard after- wards the Germans had succeeded in digging themselves into their new positions and had given our chaps hell. At all events we lost heavily in officers and men. Among the missing was Gilbert's company commander—he who had returned to the battalion shortly before the battle of Arras and to whom I had thereupon become second-in-command, though I had commanded the company in action, as he had been ordered to remain behind. I was hoping that Gilbert would be given command of B Company. But I was not surprised when someone else was appointed. Dawson never thought much of Gilbert's executive powers. I think he was probably right. Gilbert was brave (which is not the same as saying that he was fearless) and devoted in carrying out his orders and in caring for his men. But bravery and devotion could not make up for his spasms of forgetfulness. He was not a natural commander. If he had been, I doubt if I should have had the same affection for him. I have never felt drawn to 'natural commanders'.

The battalion, or what was left of it, was withdrawn into the support trenches and we who had remained behind went up to join them. We stayed there, near the south bank of the Scarpe, for two or three weeks. It was during this period that we sat under some of the heaviest artillery bombardments that had so far come my way. There were no dugouts in the trenches which we occupied. The only protection was a sheet of corrugated iron placed over the trench and heaped with earth or sandbags. Some of the men undercut the trench so as to make little cubby holes for themselves and in this way gained some slight protection. Though the practice of undercutting was strictly forbidden because it increased the danger of being buried alive, yet on this occasion it was impossible (and I did not try) to prevent it. The men stood a pretty good chance of being buried alive whether they undercut the trench or not. Undercutting did at least give them something to do while they were being shelled.

The worst kind of shell from the point of view of morale— that is, for breaking your spirit—was 'the crump', the high-explosive shell which burst above ground in a shattering, wrenching blast of black smoke and almost blew the breath out of your body. This shell usually did little material damage. Corrugated iron covered with earth would, with luck, protect you from the splinters. But the effect of this form of ballistic on your outlook was depressing. A little of it went a long way. After half-an-hour of it you began to have a headache, or at least a moral headache —if that means anything.

The real material damage—the damage to persons and property, as the lawyers say—was done by the shell that burst on contact. The heaviest German shell that ever came my way (I managed to avoid it) measured fourteen inches across the base. There was a period when a few of them were fired into Arras at nine o'clock in the morning. I always thought that was a good example of German precision—and of German stupidity. Every morning at nine o'clock precisely the shells would come across. That went on for about a fortnight without variation. They all of them fell round about the same spot, and were fired, so we were told, from a gun somewhere near Douai, which gun could also fire up into the Ypres salient. I pictured it on a railway triangle, firing at Arras at nine o'clock in the morning and at Ypres, say, at two o'clock in the afternoon. There may have been some particular target which they were after at Arras. If so, I never knew what it was. All I do know is that the shells never did any serious military damage. They made great craters and they knocked down buildings. But no one was living in that part of the city and once you knew where and when these shells were going to fall it was easy to fix things so that never the time and the place and the loved one were altogether. The reason I know the calibre of those shells is that one of them failed to explode. This one I examined (carefully) and measured.

But shells like that were rare. For strafing the P.B.I. in the trenches shells of a very much smaller calibre were used. They were quite effective enough. The worst part of a bombardment, I found, was the beginning, when you did not know where the next shell would fall. After a time and provided you lived as long, you had the bombardment, so to speak, taped. You knew where the shells were falling and almost when they were due. I remember well being in one bombardment which lasted for several hours and after the first quarter of an hour we knew where every shell in our immediate neighbourhood was going to fall and the length of the intervals between their falling. There was one in

particular which fell nearer to us than the rest. When it was due
we would lie flat : and we so judged the time that we were never
down for more than about half-a-minute before our friend
arrived. Of course there were inaccuracies in the fire and the
shell which fell near us might well have fallen on us. But that was
a question of luck. So far as artillery bombardments went I was
very lucky.

One curious thing about most bombardments was the way they
invariably destroyed latrines. It almost seemed that the Germans
were bent (with what sinister purpose you may imagine) on making the life of our sanitary squads a burden.

But to me the worst feature of these bombardments was the
sound of men shouting and the sight of men running with
stretchers. If you could hear the words that were shouted (usually
'Stretcher-bearers! Stretcher-bearers!') the strain was less on the
imagination. But when you heard shouting and could not distin-
guish the words, the pictures you thought up were infinite and
dreadful. And somehow the sight of men running, even if they
were carrying stretchers and you knew why they were running,
had a baleful effect. If they carried no stretchers and had no
obvious reason for hurry, the effect was still worse, so that I would
shout at them and order them to stop.

The acrid smell produced by the explosion of a shell did not
trouble me. The smell of a dead horse was infinitely worse. But
ever since those days, on the occasions when I have sniffed exploded gunpowder, it has always brought back memories of sitting in a trench and being shelled.

Gilbert and I were not together at this time, though we were
not far apart. The worst of it was that I did not know what was
happening to him. Just after a bombardment, word came that he
had been blown up. But almost immediately afterwards a note
arrived from Gilbert himself (I have it still) which said that 'all
that happened was that I encountered a 5.9 along Long Lane
which jerked me skywards and completely buried me. I got out
all right and am now absolutely fit, tho' it gave me a bit of a head
from concussion.'

VIII

It was at this period, just after we had been moved back from the support line to the reserve line, that a case of attempted mutiny occurred—the only case that ever came my way.

A large dump of trench props (actually railway sleepers, which could be used for the same purpose) had been assembled a mile or so back from the reserve line we were holding. On our first evening in that line my company was ordered to fetch those sleepers and take them up to the support trenches which had been heavily shelled and where in consequence props were badly needed. The job had of course to be done by night. As it began to get light soon after three in the morning this did not leave us too much time. The men, who had had a pretty gruelling time and were looking forward to a good night's rest, were not over-joyed at being turned out for a fatigue. However the job had to be done and as soon as darkness fell we started off.

There were about a hundred of us altogether. The journey itself was an abomination. The ground was pitted with shell-holes, so that we had to clamber in and out of them and often took headers when they were least expected. And when we reached the place where the dump was supposed to be, we couldn't find it. The spot had been marked on my map at the foot of a railway embankment. We found the embankment but searched in vain for the dump. Meanwhile the men were getting more and more fed up and time was running on. At last we discovered that the dump was not where it had been marked on the map but on the further side of the embankment. This meant that we had to scramble up the bank and down the other side. The banks were high and steep. Nor were the men any better pleased when they realised that their first job would be to scramble back over the bank again, each carrying a sleeper.

I gave the company a five-minutes breather. Then each man got hold of a sleeper and we started back. It is difficult to say which was more tiresome—scrambling up the bank with a sleeper on your shoulder or slithering down the other side. All I can remember is that during the process the air was filled with a

richer variety of oaths than I had ever heard before or indeed
have heard since.

When all the men were over I gave the word to pick up sleepers
and we set off on our way in single file. Two sergeants were with
me, one in front, the other in the rear.

The difficulties of the outward journey were only a foretaste
of what we were to meet with going back. Time after time men
missed their foothold and fell headlong, with the sleepers coming
down on top of them. Before long a heavy shower of rain com-
pleted their discomfort. Now they were slipping about all over
the place, losing their grip of the sleepers, sometimes losing the
sleepers themselves.

At the end of twenty minutes, I called a halt and told the men
they could rest for five minutes. Meanwhile I was wondering how
we were going to deliver the goods. It was already half past one.
We had another hour and a half or so of darkness. Even if I
could arrange for a relief (which was doubtful) it was very uncertain whether they could be mobilised and sent to take over in
time.

At this point my thoughts were interrupted by the sound of
voices and murmurings coming from the rear. Several times I
caught the word 'relief'. I made my way back and stood for a
moment listening under cover of darkness to what was being said.
The expedition was, I soon gathered, considered a mistake—as
well as a piece of deliberate cruelty; and the sooner I was told
so the better. (This is a polite summary of the comment I heard.)

I went back to the head of the column, resolved to get a relief
as soon as I could : but knowing also that it might not be possible
to get it in time. I then gave the order to move on. The men in
the front picked up their sleepers and started going forward.
From the rear came shouts of 'What about a relief? We want a
relief! It's a bloody shame!' and so on. Above these shouts soared
the warning voice of the sergeant. 'Nah then, nah then, mind wot
you're saying! We don't want to hear no talk like that!' Whereupon there followed a lively exchange, in which the sergeant, an
old soldier, gave as good as he got.

I went along and—rather unnecessarily—asked the sergeant

what the matter was. I was answered immediately by several of the men.

'We want a relief, sir.' 'A little more o' this and we'll be done in, sir.' 'This is a job for 'orses, not for men!' There were other comments, but as they were all spoken at once I could not catch them.

It was evidently my turn to speak.

'I know you want a relief,' I said, 'and I'm going to try to get one. But we've got to get up to the reserve line first, before there's any chance of a relief. And we've got to do it quick, otherwise we sha'n't be through before sunrise. So pick up your loads and get on.'

I turned away, hoping they would do as I had told them. I had no idea what I should do if they refused. I had tried to be firm and at the same time conciliatory and had left the rest to luck—and the sergeant.

To my relief the party moved forward and for the time being I heard no more save a few round oaths.

But the route seemed longer and rougher than ever and at the end of another half-hour I was thinking that I would have to give the men another rest, in spite of the fact that time was against us and that I wanted to reach Brigade Headquarters (where I could telephone for a relief) without another halt. But the men themselves forestalled me. Someone in the rear cried 'Halt!' and without a second's hesitation the company halted, each man dropping his sleeper and himself on top of it. Seeing their condition one could hardly blame them. I think that if I had been twenty years older I should probably have shrugged my shoulders and left them resting while I went to find a relief. But in those days my sense of discipline was unimpaired. Soldiers, I felt, ought not to take the law into their own hands.

Without pausing to think of possible consequences I ordered the men to take up their loads.

Not a man stirred. All that happened was that a few shouts came from the rear: 'Give us a relief! We don't move till we get a relief!'

This was something new. Even in my callow days at Tonbridge I had never had an order questioned. Yet here in France was

faced with a sit-down strike. It was something I had not en-
visaged.

'Get up, d'ya hear!' growled one of the sergeants.

But now, as I had given a definite order, it was clearly up to
me to see that it was carried out.

'All right, sergeant, leave this to me,' I said in a voice that
suggested that I had the position in hand and knew exactly what
I was going to do—which was very far indeed from being the
case.

'D Company!' I began, addressing the men as though they
were on parade and, I hope, reminding them that they were
soldiers. 'You have been given an order and you will obey it. I
know, as well as you do, that we need help on this job, and as
soon as we get up to Brigade Headquarters, and it's not far now,
I'm going to try to get a relief for you. But whether we get a
relief or not, we're going to do our job. The sleepers that you're
carrying are wanted for the men in the line. And they're going to
have them. Fall in!'

These heroic words did not, I regret to say, have the desired
effect. I don't know what the men thought. Perhaps they were
too tired to think. All the response I got was a shout or two from
the rear that they wanted a relief and weren't going to move till
they got it.

I was now up against it. So far as words went I had shot my
bolt. And everybody knew it.

The sergeant came up to me with some sort of a suggestion.
But I did not listen.

'Very well!' I said, scarcely realising what I was saying.
'You've heard the order to fall in and I give you exactly fifteen
seconds to obey it. We're on active service now, and I've got a
loaded revolver in my hand. If any man refuses to obey I shan't
hesitate to use it.'

I spoke as though I meant it. The effect was immediate.
Muttering curses the men picked up their sleepers and moved on.

I do not look back on this incident with pride. After fifty years
of civilian life I could no more use a revolver against a man for
disobeying me (unless he was going to kill me and I had told him
not to) than I could hit him if I did use it. Nor, to be honest, do

I think that I should have used my revolver in the way I threatened to that night. If my bluff had been called I might have
caved in. I might, I suppose, have fired into the air (in which case
I might have hit one of the men, for I never fired my revolver
in France except to shoot rats: and so far as I know I never succeeded in even wounding one). The reason my bluff wasn't called
was, I think, that I spoke as though I meant it. But I learnt my
lesson—to think twice before giving a fatal order of the kind
again.

The end can be told very briefly. We reached Brigade Headquarters where I halted the men and leaving them in charge of
the sergeant, went out in search of a telephone. At the entrance
to the General's headquarters I found a sentry sitting on a pile of
sandbags. He was half-asleep and when I spoke to him he answered me casually, without shifting his position. I daresay he
was tired. But so was I . . . I didn't shoot him, but I gave him
hell.

I got through on the wire without difficulty to my own battalion and secured a relief. Before dawn the sleepers reached their
destination.

IX

The high-spot of excitement for me that year occurred on a
pleasant July day spent by us in endeavouring to 'straighten out'
the line. The operation was a very small one involving only two
half companies. I was in charge of one half-company, and
Henderson Roe, now captain of B Company, was in charge of
the other. Our objective was a line of trenches previously occupied by the British, captured about ten days previously by the
Germans and situated some five hundred yards in front of our
front line. The Army Commander had said that the trench must
be retaken at all costs.

The attack was originally planned for 4 a.m. on July 15th.
Heavy rain had fallen during the night and it was still drizzling
when we had just got into position and were standing by our
ladders. (The trenches in that part of the line were deep and we
had to have ladders in order to get out.) I was next to a man who

seemed in a bad way. He was an elderly chap who was a green-grocer by trade and had been in the Army only a few months and in France only a few weeks. This was his first experience of 'going over the top', and he clearly was a bit frightened, though he was doing his best to put on a brave face. A man of small stature, he had evidently found it difficult to get things small enough to fit him. His tunic and trousers were miles too big. So was his tin hat, which came down almost over his eyes. His boots were immense and sunk as they were in the sticky clay the man was almost a fixture. He was too a born fumbler. The chief thing that had been impressed on every man was that he should keep his rifle clean and see that its essential parts were free of mud. And here was Private Green (call him that: I forget now what his name was) with his rifle clogged with clay. 'I laid it by the side of the trench, like,' he explained with an apologetic grin, 'and when I looked round again it had fallen over.' Between us we got it into working order again and, with an extra tot of rum which the sergeant found for him out of the bottom of the jar, he was as ready for battle as it was possible to make him. In response to my enquiry he even went so far as to say that he was feeling right enough—adding however that he wished that it wasn't raining. 'Makes it a bit difficult to move, sir,' he said, 'in all this mud.'

I tried to cheer him up by reminding him that it was raining also on the Germans and that in another few minutes something worse than water would be falling on them. He grinned.

But my prophecy was not to be fulfilled. For at one minute to the hour a breathless runner arrived to announce that the attack had been postponed.

With the exception of my greengrocer friend, who was clearly relieved, the company as a whole was disappointed. It was not so much that we wanted to go over: but we were all keyed up for the job. The delay, however, enabled us to touch up our prepara-tions which had been rather hurriedly made, and also to get the men together in a large dug-out where I made them what was meant to be a rousing speech. I described to them the strength of the barrage that was going to be put down on the Germans the moment we went over—everything, ranging from trench mortars to heavies—and told them (God forgive me!) what a magnificent show it was going to be. When I asked them if they were ready for it, they cheered to the echo. The postponement, which we were told was due to bad weather, was only for forty-eight hours. So, on the morning of the 17th we went over.

Before the attack we went through the usual procedure. We synchronised our watches. We put our ladders in position. We doled out the rum. (At least we doled out most of it, for more than a due share of it went, I am sorry to say, down the throat of one of my subalterns whom I discovered two minutes before zero hour lying insensible at the bottom of the trench. There was nothing to do about it at the time. To have put him under arrest would have meant getting hold of another officer and there was no time to do that. So I left him where he was. From that day to this I have never set eyes on him, nor do I know what happened to him. I gave his sergeant charge of his platoon.)

At 5.30 precisely the bombardment began. We climbed up our ladders and went forward. It was a strange sensation walking upright in no-man's land when up till then you had only crawled. But I did not feel afraid, or at least not nearly so afraid as I had felt immediately before going over—and even then there had been so much to do that fear was not a very present feeling. But now there was so much to think about, so much to distract my attention, that I forgot to feel afraid—it is the only explanation. The noise, the smoke, the smell of gunpowder, the rat-tat of rifle and machine-gun fire combined to numb the senses. I was aware of myself and others going forward, but of little else. In one hand I carried a rifle with fixed bayonet and in the other a Mills bomb. Two things I remember very well. One was that some of our Stokes mortars were firing short—the result of using salved ammunition. I made a mental note that when I got back I would see to it that no salved ammunition was used for the future. The other was that when some smoke had cleared I found myself standing on the parapet of a trench gazing down at a pale-faced German who had his arms raised above his head and was shouting 'Kamerad!' at me. Should I have bayoneted him or thrown my bomb at him? I suppose rather that I should have taken him prisoner and handed him over to one of our own men, who would have escorted him back. As it was I did none of these things. To have taken him prisoner would have meant that one of our own men would have been lost to us for the attack. As for killing him, I could not do it. So I turned and left him, much, I think, to his astonishment.

In the confusion I have no very clear idea of what followed. I had made a careful study of the map beforehand and I knew exactly how the German trenches should have looked—I mean the lines they followed and the shape of them. But now the ground, already pitted with shell holes, had been so broken by our barrage that it was impossible to make out where the trenches were.

Picture the scene. Smoke and explosions everywhere. Bombs and hand grenades popping off all round. Figures running through the smoke. The line of attack which had started so well is a line no longer. Suddenly, away to the left, a machine-gun starts rat-tatting and then, as I wrote at the time, 'a curious thing happened. One man lost his head and turned and ran. Then another and another and although there were no Germans about, all our men retired. I tried to rally them, but only succeeded in gathering three men and three wounded corporals. We jumped in the trench and took advantage of a shell-hole which we consolidated as much as possible'. In the confusion something had happened to the attack, something that looked like retreat and failure. Yet we had come a good distance and must by now have reached our objective. But where *was* the objective? Where *were* the trenches? That trench where I saw the fellow with his hands up —perhaps *that* was the line we were aiming at. If so, I must be about level with it, though I am some distance to the right. Anyway, one takes a chance. Seeing that the machine-gun seemed to be swinging in my direction, I leapt down with the others into the shell hole and we kept a lookout till the smoke began to clear. That was the scene, as clearly as I can remember it.

Adams, the runner, was one of the men who was with us. A very sound, level-headed fellow, this Adams. I was glad to have him. Before long we were joined by Bull, a subaltern in B Company, and one of his men. Bull said he had spotted me earlier on and thought he might as well link up with us seeing that there was nobody else to link up with. The attack, so far as he could tell, had gone west—in both senses.

A little later three others found us, two corporals (both of whom were wounded, one pretty seriously in the head) and a lance-corporal, all from my company. The seriously wounded man—Corporal Donovan—had been dragged along and as we lowered him into the shell-hole he cried out with pain. We laid him down as gently as we could and so that he might have something on which to rest his wounded head we placed under it the only makeshift pillow we had—a bag of Mills bombs.

By now the din had died down, the smoke had cleared and the sun was well above the horizon. But for the war we would have been enjoying a fine July morning.

As it was we felt annoyed and rather ridiculous. We had started out to capture a particular position. Our plans had been well prepared and carefully rehearsed. We had known exactly what we were to do. Our little show was to have been a triumph of what the staff loved to call 'co-ordinated action'.

Instead, we were sitting in a shell-hole, isolated and with no idea of our position.

That was why we felt ridiculous.

Nine o'clock: and as someone observed, we had the rest of the day in front of us. What were we to do? Stay where we were? Or move out and try to make contact with our lines? We debated the question and decided that, while the rest would stay where we were, one should go back to our lines with a message. For this job the obvious man was Adams.

I wrote a note—which I have still, as it was returned to me later. It started with a rough drawing of what I thought our position might be and then gave the names of those who were with me (I put a W against the wounded). It went on:

I do not know the position of any other of our troops, but I think some of them are in the shell-holes behind us. Nearby in a shell hole lies Lt. Bristow, B. Coy., very badly wounded. He will not live. A sergeant and another man are lying dead in the same place. I wish our artillery would *lengthen range*. No sign of the Boche has been observed except in the air where he has been very active. There appear to be some aerial bombs falling near HOOK TRENCH fired from the direction of the N end of Bois du Vert.

9.10 a.m. 17.7.17.

The aerial activity I referred to was very different from the *blitzkriegs* of the second war. All that happened was that a couple of aeroplanes came circling round our neighbourhood. One of them—it was painted white—flew so low that I could see the face of the pilot. I remember feeling a curious thrill at actually seeing a German. It was, in those days, such a rare experience.

I gave the note to Adams who stuffed it into the lining of his tin-hat. He seemed very confident of being able to get back and said that no doubt we'd be seeing him again before long. He then took a couple of bombs, one of which he put in his pocket and the other he carried in his hand, and slithering out of the shell-hole, disappeared.

To enable us to keep a look-out we had clipped a small mirror on to a bayonet whose tip protruded above ground. This gave us a field of vision to the east and we took it in turns to keep watch. The rest of us either dug or slept. At midday we ate our rations, cooking some by the aid of candles.

It was about five o'clock in the afternoon when Bull, who was keeping watch in the mirror, told us there was 'something moving'. Presently a hand stretched slowly over the rim of the shell-hole. It was clasping a Mills bomb and to our relief the sleeve on the arm was not field grey but khaki.

The next instant the kindly and rather ascetic features of Henderson Roe peered down on us.

We hailed him with joy. If he had been capable of showing enthusiasm I think he would have shown it then. He did in fact go so far as to say that he was glad to find we were not Huns.

This man Henderson Roe was a strange, aloof and for most people rather a frightening creature. He had been a regular soldier and wore the South African ribbon. He had spent much of his time in a remote and unhealthy corner of the Empire and seemed to be a permanent invalid—though he never on any account went sick. How he had ever contrived to rejoin the Army and come out to France was a mystery. In fact for most of us it was difficult to understand how he managed to exist at all, seeing that he lived mostly on aspirins. His spare time he spent alone, reading. Whereas the rest of us had parcels of food sent out to us, his parcels, which were frequent, contained only books. I was a sort of friend of his (a remote and rather brittle relationship) but most people regarded him as supercilious and stand-offish— as indeed he was.

'There's no one about,' he observed. 'You can rest your rifles.'

The cool, calm way in which he spoke relieved the tension. It also made us feel more ridiculous than ever, squatting there with our rifles and bombs as though we were expecting the Boche.

Henderson Roe had been buried for eight hours. At least that was what he told us and judging from his corpse-like appearance and his grimy clothes, I have no doubt he was speaking the truth. We made him some tea which he accepted gratefully. I told him that I had sent a message back, and he judged that there was nothing for us to do but wait, passing the time as pleasantly as we could. With a pack of cards that one of us had found in a dead man's haversack, Henderson Roe and Bull played piquet.

There was not much we could do for poor Donovan. He did his best to suffer the pain in silence, but every now and then he gave a groan. Fortunately we had plenty of water (which he often asked for) as we had removed the water-bottles, as well as the haversacks with food in, from the dead bodies which were lying near us.

As for Bristow (the lieutenant mentioned in my note) he was past all help. He remained unconscious till the early evening, and then he died. We knew he was dead because the flies immediately settled round his mouth.

So the day passed. We talked, we ate, we slept and we watched. And all was quiet.

When dusk fell and we were debating what to do, an intense bombardment was suddenly put over from our side, landing much too close to us for our liking. Two minutes later the Germans replied, their shells falling to the west of us. Thus we were caught between two fires, and there was nothing for us but to lie as flat as we could in the bottom of the shell-hole and hope for the best. We were all very cheerful (so I wrote home afterwards) and sang 'When you come to the end of a perfect day'.

After half-an-hour or so our bombardment lifted and by the light of rockets which shot up from the ground all round us, we saw that some sort of an attack was on. But as the German guns were still firing, cutting us off from our own lines, there was still no object in our moving.

At the end of an hour the bombardment ceased. Some action had taken place, but what exactly had happened we did not know. As we were looking about us, wondering if the time had come for us to make a get-away, one of the men said: 'Look, sir, there's Fritz!' I looked his way and what I saw surprised me. Not ten yards from where we were squatting in our shell-hole a line of the Boches was creeping forward in single file from east to west. We could hear the creak of their equipment as they moved. We could hear them whispering to one another as they passed. One of our shells fell among them and I heard one swear in German.

We dared not move. We hardly dared breathe. The stream of them seemed endless.

Presently Henderson Roe put his mouth against my ear and in a toneless whisper said the one word: 'bombs'.

The only bombs we had now were in the bag which Donovan was using for a pillow. Noiselessly lowering myself I felt for the opening of the bag, meaning to extract a bomb or two without disturbing him. Imagine our feelings when he groaned aloud! We were certain that the Germans must have heard us. But if they did, they paid us no attention.

I managed to extract four bombs and handed two to Henderson Roe. Pressing ourselves against the side of the shell-hole we lay motionless, with a bomb in each hand, gazing up at the passing figures silhouetted against the purple darkness of the sky.

So we waited, expecting that at any moment one of the file would stray out of his line and—literally—fall upon us. But the perfect precision which seems to characterise every German military movement counted this time in our favour. Not a man strayed from the line. By the time the procession ended we were still in position, our bombs in our hands and our hearts in our mouths.

'Whew!' It was I—not Henderson Roe—who expressed my feelings. All he said was 'A hundred and twenty I counted. What did you make it?'

'I didn't count', I said. 'I should say roughly about a million. What's the next move?'

'Give them a moment or two to get clear,' he replied coolly, 'then we might as well start.'

Whatever our position may have been all day it was now clear that we were behind the German lines.

'Don't leave me.'

It was Donovan speaking from the bottom of the shell-hole.

'We won't leave you, old boy,' Henderson Roe assured him in the kindest tone that I had ever heard him use. 'You're coming on my back.'

Between us we got Donovan out and started to creep back. The bombardment was over, but rifle fire continued. Every time a rocket went up we lay motionless. We could tell from the places where the rockets were being fired how far we were behind the German lines and also where our lines were: for our own Very lights were easily distinguishable from the German rockets. A couple of hundred yards we reckoned would see us through the Boche front line. After that perhaps another hundred would bring us to our own.

The going was slow. Not only had we to halt every time a rocket went up, not only had we to go gently with Donovan, but we had also to take care not to run into the Boche. Pickets of them seemed to be dotted about at random. Every now and then a guttural conversation just ahead would warn us to alter course.

It took us an hour and a half to cover that two hundred yards. At any moment we might have collided with the Germans. At any moment Donovan's groans (he did his best to keep them down) might have given us away. Somehow we got through to no-man's land. Easy, we thought, to make our own lines now. We were wrong—for an obvious reason. We were on ground that each side was watching intently. Any movement in it aroused suspicion and drew fire. Now, instead of creeping, we crawled on our bellies, dragging Donovan along as best we could. When rockets or Very lights went up or, as happened several times, a German machine-gunner loosed off a few rounds (to make sure, Henderson Roe said, that his gun was in working order) we lay flat and motionless, our faces buried in the not so good brown earth.

But the real trouble came when we were approaching our own lines. We knew they were our own, because in the light of a rocket we saw along the skyline a row of round tin-hats—easily distinguishable from the squarer shape of the Boche tin helmet. But spotting our own boys (which we did with some relief) was not the same thing as making them understand that we were not a German patrol. We did not, I'm afraid, go about the business very sensibly. Our joy at getting clear of the Germans had made us slightly reckless. On seeing our boys (there were so many of them, they were obviously 'standing to') we gave a little cheer— which immediately drew fire from both sides, Lewis guns included. Till that moment I had often wondered what our marksmanship was really like. Now, as the Lewis gun bullets spat over my back, I came to know. At any other time I would have been glad to congratulate the gunners.

There we were, then, lying within thirty or forty yards of our own lines. If we moved (for Very lights were frequent now suspicion was aroused) we were quickly fired upon.

We tried shouting. We bawled 'West Kents!' 'Queen's Own!' 'Don't fire!' at the tops of our voices. But our words didn't carry. Or if they did, they didn't carry conviction. The result was only another burst of fire. Optimistically I tried to sing the Regimental March ('A Hundred Pipers'). I even whistled it. But the result was not what we hoped. There were no answering calls, no shouts of friendly welcome or even of challenge. All we brought upon ourselves was fire. Fire from both sides.

'I think,' I announced to Henderson Roe, 'I shall go to sleep.'

He agreed it wasn't a bad idea.

'The Boche'll probably attack in the morning,' I went on, 'and where shall we be then?'

'Here,' he replied.

'I doubt it.'

'No. You're probably right,' he said. 'We shall be blown to pieces in the preliminary barrage.'

'That's more like it,' I agreed. 'In which case this is our last night.'

'Quite likely.'

'What's a good subject to talk about,' I asked, 'on our last night?'

'What do you suggest?'

'Socrates,' I replied. 'How would he have faced it?'

I do not know why I thought of Socrates. There was no special reason—except that one had to face the situation philosophically.

'Socrates?' Henderson Roe yawned. 'Yes, he's as good a chap as any to think about. He would have agreed with the idea of going to sleep. After all, we can do no good by keeping awake. We can't get on.'

At this point Donovan groaned—and I think we both felt guilty. I know I did. We had to get on, if only for Donovan's sake.

So we crept nearer, until with unexpected suddenness a voice challenged us.

'Oo's that?'

We flattened ourselves against the ground, and shouted our names. This time our shouts were answered, not by bullets but by friendly words:

'Come on, sir! We've been lookin' for you everywhere!'

We 'came on', bringing Donovan with us, and entered our own lines.

As soon as we were in and the handshakes were over, we asked the way to battalion headquarters. Instead of going along the communicating trench we walked over the top, no longer afraid of German fire now that we were on our own ground.

In the dug-out we found Alderman who was in temporary command of the battalion, Dove the adjutant—and a German prisoner. We were welcomed as though we had come back from the dead, for they had given up hope of seeing us again. The attack, it seemed, had been considered a failure. Some of our men had been killed, more were missing and many had come back. Then at four o'clock in the afternoon Adams had turned

up with my message. He had left us at nine in the morning and
had taken seven hours to cover the few hundred yards he had
to go. The delay was due (as he told us later) to the number of
Boches he had met and just managed to avoid. Immediately the
message had been received a fresh attack had been ordered for
ten o'clock that evening—it was the preliminary bombardment
for this attack that had caught us just as we were going to leave
our shell-hole. This second attack had been a success and our
men were firmly established in the trenches they had set out to
take earlier in the day. They had had orders, Alderman said, to
look out for us, but word had come that we were nowhere to be
found. Then Bull's party had got in, reporting that we too might
be on the way. But two hours had gone by and Alderman had
pretty well given us up.

On our return we all had drinks together.

The fact was that in the original attack I and my little band
had missed our way and overshot the mark. We thus became
stranded, while the remainder, thrown into confusion by the
heavy machine-gun fire, were without a rallying point.

Donovan never recovered.

X

All that summer we were in and about Arras, sometimes in
the line, which was quiet: sometimes in reserve, which was
quieter still: sometimes in the city itself where life was normal
and civilised: and sometimes in villages south and west of the
city, which was as peaceful as living in England.

But for me a great part of that summer was spoilt because
Gilbert was not with me. Some sort of trench fever had attacked
him and for two months he was in hospital away down at Le
Tréport. We wrote to one another very often. His letters were
cheery and he always spoke of coming back 'in a week or so'. But
the weeks dragged on and it was not until the end of September
that I saw him again.

Meanwhile, on August 21st I had had a memorable interview
with Dawson. It came about this way. When we were in the line
our tea was brought up to us in sacks. Sometimes in order, I

suppose, to save time as well as sacks, the sugar would be already mixed with the tea in one sack. It was a rough and ready method, but nobody minded, provided that the tea was tea and the sugar sugar. But when, as on this occasion, the sugar turned out to be sawdust, we felt we had a grievance. The company sergeant-major reported the matter to me and produced the sack, whereupon I sat down and wrote a very rude note to the Quartermaster and sent it down to him by hand. Next morning I was sent for by the Colonel. His own groom brought a horse up to the reserve line so that no time should be lost. The business, so the groom told me, was urgent. This was an unusual procedure. I naturally wondered what was in the wind.

Half an hour later I stood before Dawson who was sitting at the entrance of his tent. Instead of giving me his usual cheery greeting, and inviting me to sit down, he frowned at me and kept me standing while he spoke.

'The Quartermaster has shown me this note which you have written,' he said sternly.

So that was it! The note I had written was rude—very rude. But it had never occurred to me that it would reach the Colonel. Even if it had, I should have thought that he would have given me his support.

'Yes, sir,' I said.

'Well? What have you got to say?' he went on in a tone which I couldn't understand. Why should I be bullied because the Quartermaster had allowed sawdust to be mixed with the tea?

'What have *I* got to say?' I repeated. 'I should have thought it was for the Quartermaster—'

'I'm not asking you what you would have thought,' cut in Dawson angrily. 'I'm asking you what you've got to say about this note.'

I was more puzzled than ever.

'Well, sir, I wrote the note,' I said, weakly. 'I don't know what there is to say about it.'

'So you think this is proper sort of language to use when addressing the Quartermaster?'

'I wrote under some provocation,' I said.

'Provocation be damned,' said Dawson. 'Language like this—'

He suddenly broke off and looked at me. Then I saw a twinkle in his eye.

'Language like this isn't half strong enough, you bloody old fool,' he exclaimed, bursting into laughter.

I was relieved, but still puzzled. Why should he have sent for me in such a hurry if he only wanted to pull my leg?

'Yours is not the only company that's been dished out with sawdust instead of sugar. There's going to be a hell of a stink about it. I'll see to that. But why I sent for you was to congratulate you.'

'To congratulate me?'

'I hear it's your twenty-first birthday today.'

I grinned at him. I had no idea that he knew.

'You'll lunch here, of course,' he went on. 'And I've got a present for you.'

I stammered inadequate thanks.

'Your leave's come through earlier than was expected. You can go tomorrow.'

I have no doubt that Dawson had seen to it that my leave came through, 'earlier than was expected'—just as he had seen to it that Veuve Cliquot was served at lunch.

That was Dawson all over.

XI

In October we left Arras and went into special training far behind the lines. We were billeted in the small village of Noeux, near Auxi-le-Château, surrounded by pleasant country, some of it wooded but mostly green stretches of open grassland—over which we manoeuvred. We were in the place for something like a month and grew attached to it. For one thing we liked the people we were billeted on—an old peasant and his wife, their daughter and granddaughter, aged eight, whose name was Gizèle. The daughter's husband was away with the army 'down south'. They were kindly folk, these peasants, and did everything they could to make us comfortable. Besides this we were a happy company. The men, brought up to full strength by fresh troops from England, were pleased at having a long spell out of the line. In the push we were preparing for it was clear that open warfare was expected. This in itself was a tonic for everyone. To snap out of the interminable trench warfare and get the Germans on the run was a splendid prospect. Now there seemed a chance of it. For under the seal of the greatest secrecy we were told that a new feature of the coming show would be an armoured vehicle known as a tank. We had seen a few of these queer, horrible-looking contraptions about already. In this new push they were, we were told, to be used in great numbers and the Boche would have a big surprise.

Our company mess too was a great success at Noeux. Mansel Carey, the mess officer, had a nice appreciation of table delicacies. The mess corporal was a grocer in civil life and consequently knew about supplies. His name was Dodd and he was never at a loss. Of him we used to say, parodying the words of a song that was popular at the time:

> Dodd will remember
> Dodd will provide.

And as our cook had been chef at one of the principal London terminus hotels, B Company mess had a reputation extending beyond the battalion.

But Noeux for me is a place of more intimate memories. Gilbert had come back and all the time we could spare we spent together. A favourite walk led up over the fields to the west, skirting the wood that bordered the main road and so down into Auxi. The church there I remember well. I picture it with Gilbert standing near the altar gazing up at the inscriptions on the walls. I remember too the *pâtisserie* Gazon, where we often had tea together. Best of all I remember the walk back over the hill—we usually went by road because of the darkness—and the times we planned to have together when the war was over.... I do not think that at any period of the war I was ever happier than I was with Gilbert at Noeux.

XII

On a day in mid-November we packed up and left. For me the journey was a sad one, not only because we were saying good-bye to a place where we had all been happy, but also because, shortly before leaving, Dawson had told me that in the coming show I was to be left out and that Gilbert would command the company. It was not, I think, that I had any fierce desire to be in the battle, though the prospect of not being in on what we thought might be a break-through and perhaps the turning point of the war was naturally disappointing. But what I really wanted was to be in the show *with Gilbert*: and failing that for Gilbert to be left out. For I knew that if he were to command the company he would forget that his place in the fight was not necessarily in front of everybody else. He would, I knew, be desperately afraid of letting the company down. He would go rushing ahead without a thought for his own safety—and anything might happen.

I put all this to Dawson and begged him, if he wouldn't let Gilbert stay behind, at least to let me go as well. He wouldn't listen—mainly, I think, because he himself, to his indignation, was being left out and had been given a job on the Divisional staff. All he promised was that he would ask the Brigadier if a place could be found for me on the Brigade staff.

The first part of the journey from Noeux was accomplished in lorries. These took us in the direction of Péronne—which was the first inkling we had of where the push was going to be. After that we took to our feet, marching by night and resting by day in heavily camouflaged bivouacs. No one was allowed out by day at all and as soon as the night's march was over the first job of the transport was to gather branches of trees or anything else they could find to put over the wagons.

We ended up at the village of Gonnelieu which lay behind a very quiet sector of the line. No-man's land at this point was over a mile wide and was thickly wired. I remember looking over the great brown stretch of tangled wire and on to the rising ground beyond, and wondering how our fellows would get by: for there was to be no preliminary bombardment. The answer apparently was that the tanks—masses and masses of them—were to go crashing through the stuff, opening up great pathways for our men, and that after a gap had been made the cavalry would go pouring through, the Boche line would be turned, and the end of the war would be in sight. It was a heartening thought—the more so as the Boche apparently had no wind of our plans. Here we were, concentrated and ready to strike, and the Boche knew nothing of it.

On the night before the attack I was sent for and told that instead of remaining behind with the battalion transport I was to act as Staff Captain to the Brigade. This was great news. It meant not only that I would have a definite job but also that I could move forward with the General and be in the best possible position to get news of what was happening. Dawson had worked this for me and I was grateful.

Meantime I was spending as much time as I could with Gilbert and my company. There was plenty to do—getting the men into position, linking them up with the flanking units, going over the trench maps and making sure that the officers and N.C.O.s knew where their objectives lay. Every now and then, as often as we were alone, I would tell Gilbert that he was to take his time, to keep his place in the centre of the company and not go rushing ahead ... I knew exactly how he felt and how ridiculously obsessed he was with the idea that he might let the company down. He was infinitely more afraid of that than he was of the Boche. Nothing I could say could shift that fear. I even had a word with the sergeant-major who, I think, understood the kind of risks that Gilbert would take. The sergeant-major, like the good old soldier that he was, promised me that he would 'keep an eye on Mr. Carré'.

The front was quiet—unnaturally so, when we remembered the ten-day bombardment before the battle of Arras. Yet the quietness was comforting. It told us that our plans were unsuspected and that the Boche was going to be taken off his guard. Besides that, there were the tanks—scores and scores of them, rolling and jerking themselves into position, like clumsy, prehistoric beasts. Sometimes they got stuck in awkward attitudes. One, I remember, broke down as it was trying to climb a steep embankment and remained with its nose in the air as if it were sniffing round for the rest of the herd. It looked so forlorn that at any moment you might have expected it to start howling for its parents.

As it happened we were near the extreme right of the line of attack. So that the Boche might be made to think that the line was longer than in fact it was, some wooden tanks had been built (looking of course like the real thing) and they were set in position to our right and stretched southward as far as we could see. It was a ruse of war that rather pleased us.

The day was the 20th of November. Zero hour was 7.30. At 7.20 I said good-bye to Gilbert. There was a wall—I think it was the wall of a farmhouse—immediately in front of the village of Gonnelieu. Behind this wall Gilbert had collected the company. The men were all in good heart and eager to get on. Gilbert and I walked along the line and I wished them all good luck. I then shook hands with him.

'Look after yourself,' I said. 'I'll see you this evening.'

He smiled and then in his queer formal way (perhaps because the men were standing near us) he saluted.

After that he went off at the head of the company, so as to get into final position for advancing when the time came. Just before he turned the corner of the wall he looked back to where I was standing and waved. I waved back.

Five minutes later the guns crashed out.

XIII

I have no clear memory of that day. Noise and the forward movement of troops are all that remain—until the afternoon, when the General decided to move forward also. We passed through the village of Flesquières and along a sunken road leading to a farmhouse known as Pam-Pam Farm and situated a few hundred yards behind Lateau Wood—over five miles in front of Gonnelieu. Just before reaching the farmhouse we turned off to the right and were led to a deep and spacious dug-out which had housed a German command. This dug-out became brigade headquarters.

On the journey up I had asked every likely person I met for news, especially for news of our battalion. From all I could hear the advance had gone well—'according to plan'. 'Our boys have got Jerry on the run this time', one man told me, adding that we were probably in Cambrai by now. I asked him if there had been any heavy fighting. Not much, he thought, though there might have been a bit of scrapping up by Lateau Wood.

Lateau Wood had been one of our objectives, one of the places my company was supposed to take.

I plodded on. I did not like the sound of that 'bit of scrapping up by Lateau Wood'. I felt sure that our chaps had been in it, and that Gilbert had been in it, too.

At seven o'clock in the evening I got more definite news. It came from one of our battalion runners whom I spotted among the crowd at our headquarters. Our chaps, he said, had 'copped it badly'.

'It was just this side of Lateau Wood,' he told me. 'Old Jerry made a bit of a stand and they say the major's been knocked out, and a few others as well.'

'Major Alderman?'—he who was commanding the battalion.

'Yes, sir. So they say.'

'And who of the others?' I asked quickly.

'Mr. Bourchier and Mr. Gow, for two.'

The man hesitated, trying to remember what he had been told.

'And Mr. Carré?' I asked. 'Is there any news of Mr. Carré?

'Yes, sir. He's one of them.'

'Mr. Carré,' I repeated. 'You don't mean Mr. Carey?'

'No, sir, I think Mr. Carey's all right.'

'You mean it's Mr. Carré who's been killed?' I carefully distinguished between the pronunciation of the two names.

'That's what they say, sir.'

There was only this man's word. But I knew that what 'they' had said was true.

And so it was.

The next morning I saw Gilbert—lying on the ground. He had been carried from the place where he had fallen—near Lateau Wood—to the ruins of Pam-Pam Farm. In his eagerness he had rushed ahead of his men, careless of his safety. He had been killed instantly by a bullet through the heart. There was hardly any trace of the wound on his uniform, beyond a small hole. His eyes were closed and his features were calm and unaltered.

His pockets had already been emptied by the stretcher-bearers,

but they had left his whistle which still hung by a strap from one
of the buttons of his tunic. It was one of the whistles I had
handed out to him at Noeux and for which he had given me a
receipt ('Received four sirens'—I have that receipt still). I un-
fastened the whistle and did the tunic button up again.

For a little while I stood looking down at him, trying to understand what had happened.

Then I came away.

XIV

Fortunately I had no time to think. My chief job was to see
that the three battalions in the Brigade were supplied with
rations. These were carried up from the rear on mules. Every
evening just as it was getting dark I had to meet the mules and
guide them to Brigade headquarters, where the rations were
checked over and then sent on their way to the battalions. It was
a long business—especially when the Boche started shelling. As
often as not dawn was breaking before the job was finished.

During the day I had to trot round with the General, sometimes going round the line, sometimes attending Divisional conferences, and always making notes and seeing that the General's
instructions were understood and carried out. A queer man was
this General. At times he could be very jovial and good-humoured.
One of his more fanciful fads, I remember, was the way he used
nautical terms. When he wanted an orderly, he would call for a
'marine', to go up the 'companion' and fetch something from
'the top deck'. On his door was a notice, 'Captain's Cabin'—and
on our door 'Ship's Office'. The mess-waiters were 'stewards' and
so on. That was one side of him—the bluff and hearty side. But
his temper was quick and he was by nature exceedingly impatient. Any instruction he gave he expected to see carried out
immediately. 'Have those bodies buried!' he rapped out one
morning as on our way to the line we came upon two corpses. A
note, I knew, would not fit the occasion. What he wanted was
immediate action. There was nothing for it but to collar the first
two men I saw and order them to bury the bodies. (They were on
their way down the line, these men, and were pretty pleased with
themselves—until they were suddenly turned into gravediggers.)

But the worst eruption of this General's temper occurred during Gilbert's funeral. Five of our officers were buried that day, Alderman, Gilbert and three others. They were buried in a common grave. The funeral service was held at seven-thirty in the morning. A little knot of us, including the General, stood by the side of the grave while the Padre read the service. He was a nervous little man, the Padre, and his voice reminded one of a stage curate's. That in itself was enough to irritate the General (and the rest of us, too, for the matter of that). Also it happened to be raining and we all of us wanted our breakfast—mitigations but not excuses for the General's outburst.

'Ashes to ashes, dust to dust,' quoth the Padre, taking up a handful of earth and scattering it upon the first body.

'Ashes to ashes, dust to dust,' he repeated, taking up another handful of earth and scattering it upon the second body.

The General shifted from one foot to the other and heaved a very audible sigh.

'Ashes to ashes, dust to dust,' began the Padre, stooping for yet another handful of earth.

The General exploded.

'That's the third time you've said that!' he exclaimed. 'Why must you keep repeating yourself?'

Even the tough ones among us were shocked at this interruption of the funeral service. We took deep breaths and looked down our noses.

The Padre made a feeble attempt to stand his ground.

'The Church ordains, sir,' he said, 'that those words shall be spoken over each body.'

The General shrugged his shoulders.

'Get on with it,' was all he said.

To his shame the Padre funked the rest. Forsaking the ordinances of the Church he scattered his last handful of earth upon the three remaining bodies, hurrying through the words as best he might. In another two minutes the service was over.

I walked back with the General in silence.

At breakfast he turned to me suddenly and said:

'You think I was right, don't you, Thomas, to stop that fellow repeating himself like that?'

Fortunately, before I could answer, he retracted the question. 'Oh, well. I daresay I was a bit impatient,' he grumbled. 'Let's forget it.'

I didn't mind much what he had done. Nothing that anybody did or said could have affected me much at that time.

XV

On the night of the 29th Hodgson-Smith came back from leave. He looked in to see me on his way up to the battalion and spoke very sympathetically of Gilbert. At what must have been heavy cost to his natural reserve and lack of sentiment he said that though I had lost Gilbert I had still got him. Which touched me a lot. He then told me about the shows he had been to in town—this by way of cheering me up. I listened as attentively as I could because I did not want to hurt his feelings. He left me about ten o'clock.

Later that evening I managed to take a look at my company who were disposed round the eastern edge of Lateau Wood. In spite of the bad conditions and the weather—it was raining hard that night—the men were in good health and in good heart. They were also glad of the rum I dished out to them. 'Puts new life into you, sir,' one man remarked after he had drained his tot.

Before leaving I talked things over with Mansel Carey who was now in command of the company. We both had the feeling that something should be happening. After all the attack had succeeded. A hole had been knocked in the German line. It was even reported that our chaps were in the suburbs of Cambrai. What we had expected to see were masses of troops and guns and tanks pouring through the gap and turning the Boche line. Instead, here we were sitting still, digging in as though we were preparing for trench warfare—and no sign of anyone following up the break-through. Carey supposed the brass-hats knew what they were up to and thought that we should 'see something' before long. I said I hoped so—and that was the last word I ever spoke to him.

Before long we did 'see something'. But not what we expected.

XVI

At eight o'clock the next morning—the morning of the 30th November—I was shaving in the deep dug-out that was Brigade headquarters. I had finished lathering and was just getting busy with the razor, when a great gust of air was blown down the entrance. It was caused by the bursting of a shell. Another shell followed, then another and another. The Boche, it seemed, was staging a bombardment—the first he had put up since our arrival. The next moment an orderly came rushing down the steps with the news that the Boche was attacking.

'They're on top of us!' he shouted.

I went up and found that he was right. A field-grey figure was lying at the entrance to our dug-out—dead. A furious bombardment was going on but most of the shells were falling well behind us. The German who was lying at my feet as I stumbled out of the dug-out was evidently one of the advance-guard.

'Get your tunic on, Thomas, and come with me!' It was the General speaking. He was standing on top of the little trench which led to our dug-out, looking at Lateau Wood through his field-glasses.

I was in my braces and my face was half-lathered and half-shaved.

I dived down as quickly as I could, seized my tunic and my revolver and came up again just as the General was striding off towards the front. One of our battalions was in reserve. Colonel Smeltzer was commanding it, an old soldier, keen as mustard and as brave as they make them, but seemingly without phlegm. On reaching his headquarters we found Smeltzer giving orders right and left and so preoccupied that he didn't appear to have time for the General.

The little colonel saluted, but continued to give orders.

'Listen to me, Smeltzer,' commanded the General, 'I want you to deploy your men so that two companies are...'

He began to explain what the dispositions were to be. But the colonel was only half attending. His eyes were roving over the landscape and every now and then he turned away from the General to see what was going on.

Knowing the General's temper I could have given Smeltzer a word of advice. But that was not my job.

Then it came—as I knew it would.

'Damn you, sir, stand to attention when your General is speaking to you!'

The Germans were now only five hundred yards away and advancing in hordes. But the General's words counted for more than any Germans. They awoke in the colonel far-off memories of the barrack square when obedience to your superior officer took precedence of every other loyalty—even of your obedience to God.

'Stand still, sir!'

The colonel stood still—his eyes unwaveringly fixed on those of the General, his thumbs in line with the seams of his breeches. I also stood still—but, unlike the colonel, I had half an eye cocked at the advancing Germans.

Having dealt with Smeltzer we returned to Brigade headquarters where it soon became clear that the troops in front of us and on our right flank were having a bad time, and that if the headquarters was to be defended we ourselves should have to defend it. We had a few men at Brigade headquarters—cooks, signallers, some bandsmen doing duty as batmen, runners and mess waiters—about twenty in all, I suppose. The General put me in charge of them and told me to counter-attack if I could, or failing that to hold my ground.

Most of the men had rifles and those that hadn't turned out with whatever they could lay their hands on. One bandsman I noticed carried nothing more deadly than his fife. The cook—to his surprise—found himself in possession of a Lewis gun.

I got the men into an extended line and we advanced about twenty yards. Then a machine-gun opened fire on us and we lay down. We could see the Germans quite plainly ahead of us. They were coming on in close formation making easy targets for our Lewis gun. I told the cook, who happened to be lying next to me, to get busy. Unfortunately he hadn't the faintest idea how the gun worked. He was a north country man, this cook, of immense proportions and a cheerful disposition. In any other circumstances he would have joked about his uselessness. As it was, he came as near to being worried as the resilience of his temper would allow.

'Blamed if I know how the dratted thing works, sir,' he said, apologetically, as he handed the gun to me. 'I never did understand machinery.'

We got the gun firing and momentarily held up the advance.

Then I lifted my head, to see what the chances were of our going forward again. Instead, I received a stunning blow in the jaw—as though a heavyweight boxer had caught me with an upper cut. Blood was falling on to my tunic—and I realised that I had been wounded. I think I must have passed out for a little. When I turned over I found that I was lying in the Brigade headquarters trench with my servant, Lavender, bending over me. My jaw was now covered with a field dressing, placed there by I know not whom—probably by Lavender.

'D'you think you can walk, sir?' asked Lavender. 'The General says I'm to take you down.'

I got up on to my feet and felt all right. I asked how the men were doing and Lavender said they were doing fine. I asked who had the Lewis gun. He couldn't say. As we were talking the General turned up and asked me how I felt. I told him I was all right and argued with him for a time, speaking as best I could without moving my jaw. Then he ordered me to get out of it and told Lavender to see me as far as the Casualty Clearing Station.

So we turned our backs on the Germans and left.

XVII

We had walked about a couple of miles, Lavender and I, when I began to feel hungry and Lavender said he would see if he could find me something to eat. While I waited for him I saw a curious sight—the British Army being taken off its guard. The German counter-attack, delivered on November 30th, had been the result of expert staff work on their part and it had taken us all completely by surprise—not least our own staff. Just as up at our Brigade headquarters we had had to gather what men we could to ward off the attack, so here behind the front the order of the day was 'improvise!' Our job in front had been easier,

because we at least had seen the enemy and known that the only
thing to do was to fire at him. Back here you could only guess
at what was happening. Rumour had it that our line had been
broken and that the Boche would arrive at any moment. That
was why staff officers were rushing about in pyjamas, giving what
orders they could to what men they could find. That was why
a battalion of Guards who were marching back to rest were suddenly turned about and ordered to take up their positions again.
That was why the Corps Commander sent up a detachment of
cavalry to act as personal bodyguard to our Divisional Commander (who promptly dismounted them and, much to their
disgust, sent them to fight as infantrymen up the line). It was
on this occasion that a gunner officer in our division won the
V.C. for saving his guns.

Meanwhile I with my wounded jaw was waiting for Lavender
to bring me food. Porridge, I thought (I couldn't manage anything hard) would go down pretty well. Not that I had any hope
of porridge, but it was a pleasant thought. Stew (with not too
much hard meat in it) was the most I could expect.

Presently Lavender turned up. He brought with him neither
porridge nor stew, but an army biscuit—the kind of biscuit you
could use for hammering in nails if you didn't happen to have a
hammer handy. I was too grateful for all the help Lavender had
given me to tell him what I thought of him. But from the look
I gave him I think he must have had an inkling.

At the Casualty Clearing Station I said good-bye to Lavender.
I had been with the battalion for fourteen months without a
break and for those fourteen months I had had my place in the
scheme of things. I had been part of a unit and had had a background as well as a command. And so long as Lavender had
been with me I had felt myself to be someone. I had belonged.
Now, having shaken hands with him and wished him good luck
and turned my back on him, I came unstuck. I was anyone or
no one: a casualty to be cared for and sent home...

No sooner had I been allotted a bed in the C.C.S. than I was
whisked on to an operating table. A powerful light was shone on
my face and the last I remember was a voice asking me if I had
any false teeth.

When I came to I was in bed again. Clasped in my hand I found a piece of cotton wool—with a hard centre. The surgeon who had removed it from my jaw was responsible for this memento—a small but jagged piece of shrapnel.

XVIII

London. Queen Alexandra's Military Hospital, Millbank. My mother and father tiptoe over to my bed, which is one of twenty or so in a large ground floor ward. They think I am hovering between life and death—until I tell them that there isn't much the matter with me: only a fracture of the jawbone which will take a few weeks to get right. They are astonished to hear me speak—astonished and relieved.

For the next four weeks I am in the hospital and on the whole miserable, because I have time to think. From a world of excitement, activity and comradeship I have suddenly been transported into a world of monotony, immobility and loneliness. My mother and father come to see me almost every day. And I have other visitors—in particular Mrs. Forester whose photograph I have often seen in Hodgson-Smith's pocketcase. She is very sympathetic and kind. She brings me flowers and grapes. But all she really wants to talk about is Hodge—which is natural. But Hodge, as a topic of conversation, is not inexhaustible. We tend to go round in circles. The trouble is that she has not heard a word from him since he went back from leave and she is getting worried. I tell her all I know: that I saw him the night before the Boche attack, as he was on his way up to the battalion, but that I had had no word of him since. I promise to make inquiries. I write to various people for news of him. All I discover, after two weeks, is that he is missing, which doesn't make things any more cheerful when Mrs. Forester comes to see me. But she is very kind.

Also I get a grand letter from Meyrick Carré—sympathising with me over Gilbert's death and counselling courage. Of Meyrick's three brothers one had died before the war: another, who was an airman, had crashed and been buried at Hebuterne: and now Gilbert, the last of the three, had been killed at Cambrai. If

Meyrick's own spirit had failed him (he was Gilbert's twin) no one could have blamed him. As it was his courage seemed to overflow. The surplus of it he was offering to me. They were like that, the Carré family. His mother and father were the souls of bravery. I went to see them as soon as I was well enough to get about. They lived in a small house at East Grinstead. I remember the walk from the station to their house. The snow was thick on the ground, deadening footfalls and promoting melancholy. I wondered what sort of people I was to meet. Gilbert had spoken of his mother, of the way everyone loved her—not only the family and friends but also the people round about, the people in the village. His father had been the rector of Smarden in Kent, but now he had retired and they were living at East Grinstead in a house next door to some of their children and grandchildren.

After I had been with her a bit I was not surprised that everyone loved Mrs. Carré. She had a strong sense of humour. She was happy and was never ruffled. Also she was a devout Christian. She greeted me with a quiet friendliness which showed at once that I was not going to be embarrassed by any emotional scenes. She was, so to say, in command of herself : yet if that conveys that she was a commanding sort of person or a hard person it is a wrong description. Tears rolled down her cheeks when I told her what I knew of the way that Gilbert had died. They were tears of sorrow, not of bitterness. She did not cry out against fate or the Germans, as some people did who had lost their children. She thought of the war as a tragedy that had befallen all mankind—friend and foe alike. Just as her faith in God was unshakeable, so she accepted what He decreed without question or complaint.

I saw Mr. Carré too. He was in bed with an illness of which he eventually died. He also was a gentle, God-fearing man. I can picture him now leaning up in bed, with his ear cupped in his hand, listening to the story of Gilbert's last battle. When it was over he shook his head slowly, as an old man does who has only half-understood what he has heard. But he was very grateful (he said) to me for having come and before I went he gave me a little book he had written on the Art of Prayer.

The grandchildren, Gilbert's nieces—Hilary, Margaret and Lorna—helped that day to take our thoughts away from war.

XIX

As soon as I was well (I suppose about late February or March) I was sent to the Reserve Battalion at Tunbridge Wells. Peace-time soldiering was a strange business after France. New methods of parade-drill, the Colonel's own particular fads, did not appeal to me: and because I neglected them I was hauled up after my first week or so in front of the C.O. and told that while I was there I must conform to the customs of the battalion. He wasn't harsh with me—the Colonel, I mean. He talked to me rather like a father.

'I think I know what you feel,' he said. 'You don't want to stay with us, do you?'

I admitted that I did not.

'It's just as you like, you know. If you want to stay in England for a bit I can easily arrange it. After all, you've had a pretty good dose in France. There's no reason for you to hurry back—unless you want to.'

I thanked him and said that I wanted to go back to my battalion. There was nothing heroic about this. It was simply a feeling I had. It sprang, I think, from the fact that soldiering in France was a much freer and less formal affair than it was in England. Besides, I had a company waiting for me over there, whereas here I was a supernumerary with no particular function. The Colonel understood all this very well and promised to hasten my departure. He closed the interview by saying that if I cared to take a week or two's leave straight away he would not object.

'In fact,' he added, 'there's no need for you to hang about here if you don't feel like it. Clear off—and we'll send for you when we want you.'

His attitude was so generous that I felt ashamed—and said so. I told him I would be very happy to stay with the battalion if I was wanted and that I would be more careful about the local rules. All he said was: 'Get along while the going's good. We'll soon get you back if we want you.'

So I got along.

XX

It was not till May that I returned to France.

There was the usual sojourn at the base camp at Etaples. Here is a description I wrote to my mother in a letter dated May 8th, 1918:

The dry dusty roadways through the camp are always crowded with men of different classes hailing from all parts of the world, the plain British Tommy (not seldom accompanied by a 'Waac'), the kilted Scotsman (nearly always cracking a joke, or having the last word with a pal about half a mile away, whose name is always 'Jock'), loosely-clad Chinamen, Siamese, Indians, New Zealanders, Canadians, South Africans, gentlemen from Palestine, Negroes and Portuguese—those are just a few. They are all seemingly very cheerful and they are all whistling one tune, namely, 'Roses of Picardy'. Just near is the station—or rather siding. It is always full of trains and smoking engines—coming in or going out, day and night: and as each train goes out you hear the little horn of the French guard blowing blasts: the blasts on the horn seem as essential to the movement of the train as the steam in the engine. The place is one huge swiftly-flowing river of men and I seem to have landed in a backwater.

When at length I reached the battalion I found a temporary Colonel in command, a man I didn't know: and among the other officers a great many new faces. Fresh drafts of men and N.C.O.s had filled the gaps since Cambrai—so that the battalion, reformed, re-equipped and generally furbished up, was scarcely recognisable. More than ever, now that I was back in France, did I miss Gilbert.

I suppose it must have been a combination of wretchedness, loneliness, trench fever and mustard gas that brought me down. For early in June I collapsed and was carried away to hospital. I remember lying on a stretcher outside a convent and being stroked on the forehead by a Canadian nurse who mistook me for a wounded hero. After that I don't remember much till I was in a Red Cross train bound for the coast. In the middle of the night the train stopped because German bombers were about. We could hear the deep droning of their engines above us and the crashing of their bombs. Some of the chaps in the train were naturally restive and I remember the splendidly calm way the nurses walked slowly up and down the central corridor, reassuring everyone by their quiet refusal to get rattled and the efficiency with which they attended to our needs. I was in a top bunk next to the roof. I did my best to control my sense of fright. But I couldn't help wishing that I had been in one of the lower bunks.

After a week or so in hospital at Rouen (where the young and very personable nurses were just what were wanted for the convalescent stage, but were less suitable for my particular complaint, involving as it did intimacies of a rather embarrassing kind) I was shipped to England. This time, instead of being sent to a miliary hospital, I landed up at a V.A.D. nursing home, known before the war as the Endsleigh Palace Hotel. Here the regime was much less strict than it had been at Millbank. I had a private room to myself, daintily furnished and kept well stocked with flowers. It was in this room that Dawson came to see me. He had just recovered from his latest wound and over a plate of strawberries he told me how much he looked forward to getting back to the battalion. Dawson, as a rule, had very little use for people who were ill. A wound he could understand : something more than willpower was needed to mend a broken leg or fractured spine. But sickness, in his view, was nine times out of ten nothing but weakmindedness and if you *wanted* to get well, you could. However, he gave no sign that he felt that way about my particular complaint (whatever it was) and when he left me he said that on no account was I to hurry back. As for himself he hoped to be off in a week or two.

That was in June. By July I was well enough to go on leave. Charles Jeffries, as it happened, was also due for a holiday about this time. He was now in the Colonial Office where the loss of his vocal chords did not prevent him from holding the Empire together. He and I arranged a fishing holiday at Howtown, on Ullswater, where we spent a peaceful fortnight. We caught few fish but had fun on the lake. In between times I read Plato's *Republic*. Also Keats.

XXI

After another spell at Tunbridge Wells I left England again on September 14th to return to the battalion. This time it was Dawson that drew me back. For myself I would not have cared much whether I stayed or went. The end of the war was nowhere in sight and so far as many of us could see there was no particular reason why it should ever end. A cushy job at home at any rate for a time might have been agreeable—but for Dawson. That one of his officers should ease himself into a cushy job at home when he was fit to rejoin the battalion in France was not to be imagined. You might have thought as soon of deserting or of giving yourself a wound. The only question was how soon could you get back.

On the platform at Victoria I happened to run across Harry Barnard. Barnard had been with one of the West Kent Territorial battalions—a battalion which for years had been ready and all keyed up to be sent abroad. They had done all their training: they were fully equipped: they had nourished an *esprit de corps* (so Barnard, who was the adjutant, always used to say) of which any battalion in the army might be proud: the officers knew their men and the men their officers. There was no more compact or efficient unit in the country than this particular battalion. Several times they had been on the point of embarking for France and each time their excursion had been cancelled. At last, in the early weeks of 1918, still hoping that their turn might come— they had been disbanded. Officers and men were scattered through the different battalions in the regiment and the glory had departed. Poor old Barnard, who had fetched up with the Reserve Battalion at Tunbridge Wells, was beyond all comfort. Nothing could lift him from his state of disillusion. Now, instead of shepherding his flock abroad, here he was, himself a lost sheep.

I hailed him on the platform and he introduced me to his father, an eminent K.C., who was seeing him off. I asked Harry if he knew what battalion he was going to. He shook his head. He neither knew nor cared.

XXII

I found the battalion on the Somme, in front of Epèhy. All August they had been having a sticky time, attacking and being counter-attacked and suffering heavy losses. At the moment the line at this point was more or less stable, but the nights were enlivened by trench bombing raids. Fierce little affairs they were too—so it was said : for when I reported for duty Dawson sent word back that I was to stay behind with the Transport until the battalion came out of the line. Thus I heard about these bombing raids but was never in one. At least two of our officers were killed this way, one a newly joined subaltern who arrived the day after I did. I welcomed him at the Transport—a nice lad he was, scarcely more than a schoolboy and terribly keen. He went up the line the same night and two days later I heard that he was dead.

It was while I was with the Transport that Harry Barnard turned up. He had been posted to the 6th (which they had told him at the Base was known as the Fire-eating Battalion). I showed him round a bit and told him what he would want in the way of kit and equipment in the line. I remember particularly saying that he ought to take a second pair of socks. As it happened he too came in for some of the bombing raids and though he wasn't wounded I could see by the look of him when he came back that his first experience of warfare hadn't been too pleasant. But he was absurdly grateful for the advice I had given him, especially about the socks. He said in fact that I had saved his life. Years after the war when at his suggestion I had become a member of Gray's Inn (he got Lord Justice Duke to be one of my sponsors, and while I was eating my dinners Mr. Barnard— Harry's father—invited me to dine at the High Table with the Benchers) Harry (himself then a Judge) would introduce me to to his friends as 'the man who saved my life'.

Early in October we left the Somme and took over the line north of Arras, opposite Lens. We had been in some pretty quiet sectors in our time, but never in one so quiet as this. The silence —that is what it amounted to—was unnatural. Even when we showed ourselves above the parapet no one fired at us.

It was at this time, about a third of the way through October, 1918, that we first began to feel that the war was nearing its end. Various rumours were reaching us—such as that Austria was on the point of collapse and that Turkey was giving in—and some official announcements were circulated warning us that on no account were we to imagine that peace was in the offing. It was clear to us then that the end was not far off.

Then one day in the middle of October the great advance began.

We had the order to leave our trenches and go forward. At first we went gingerly, not knowing what to expect. The German trenches in front of us were empty. So were the support and reserve lines—all empty. By degrees we went forward with more confidence. But we very soon found that though the Boches had fled they had left a lot of little things behind them. The door of a German dug-out would be found shut, and the fellow who opened it would be blown to pieces. Trip wires were encountered, linked up with high explosives. Delayed action mines would be laid under houses—the kind of houses that would naturally be chosen as brigade or divisional headquarters. In one house a piano (always a popular find for the troops) had been left intact. When the first chord was struck up went the piano and the house as well. We soon learnt to be careful.

The brigades 'leap-frogged' one another, moving forward all the time. This was coal-mining country, dotted with great slag-heaps, in some of which the Germans had built dug-outs and shelters. The first lot of towns we passed through were nothing but ruins. Lens was a heap of rubble and twisted iron. As we advanced the towns and villages became more recognisable. In Henin-Liétard the houses were in ruins, but you could at least make out their size and shape (it was in the cellar of one of these houses that I had my argument with Dawson on democracy). Further on we found houses that were standing but heavily scarred by our artillery.

October 18th : our battalion's turn to take the lead again. A crisp morning with a heavy white mist on the ground so that you could not see ten yards in front of you. My company formed the advance guard. The 'point' (marching twenty-five yards ahead of everybody else) consisted of a sergeant and one man. Half an hour after we started I joined them, just to see how it felt to be leading the whole British Army in the direction of Berlin. The bite in the air had a tonic effect and the stolidity of the sergeant, next to whom I marched, added to one's confidence. The ring of our footsteps on the road must have told anyone who heard them that we knew where we were going and that we meant to get there...

Suddenly out of the mist a tenor voice challenged us.

'*Halt! Wer da?*'

We paused for a second and then the sergeant spoke.

'Oo are yer?'

A shot cracked. The bullet must have passed between me and the sergeant—about the level of our heads.

'Tell the men to get into the ditches', I said. We took to them ourselves, blessing the French for their sagacity in lining their *routes nationales* with ready-made trenches. We opened a covering fire with rifles and Lewis guns at point blank range. For a moment or so our fire was returned by a Boche machine-gun. Our men kept their heads down and their fire up. Then the machine-gun gave over and a moment or so later I blew my whistle and ordered the 'cease fire'. Gingerly we got up out of our ditches and advanced along the road. There was no more firing now and no more tenor voices challenging us. When we had gone about fifty yards we came to a farmhouse, situated at a cross-roads. Three or four Germans were lying there—all dead. Fading into the distance we could hear the clatter of hooves. Of the machine-gun there was not a trace. The Germans in fighting their rear-guard action were using mounted machine-guns. They held up the advance as long as they could, then galloped away.

It was here that one of our fellows removed an Iron Cross from the tunic of a dead German and presented it to me.

Having cleaned up this machine-gun post without loss to ourselves we sent back word that all was clear and then continued the advance.

We were now approaching the village of La Jonquière. The Germans were still holding the place (but not, we gathered, in any great numbers) and were covering the road leading to it with machine-guns. We crept along the ditch at the side until we came opposite the first house in the village. (Had we known that the first house would be on the right of the road we should not have chosen the left hand ditch to creep along.) The house, unlike any that we had seen up to now, had the appearance of being occupied. Awaiting our chance a sergeant and I dashed across the road. As we reached the other side the machine-guns in the village opened up again. The door of the house was bolted and we hammered on it. Presently we heard footsteps inside. A moment later the door was opened a couple of inches and an old French peasant's wizened face was staring out at us. It was plain that he had no notion who we were. Instead of flinging open the door and letting us in, he continued to stare at us through the chink.

'Come on, mister!' exclaimed the sergeant, preparing to put his weight against the door.

'*Nous sommes les Anglais!*' I announced, hoping that my accent would not be too obscure for him.

'*Les Anglais!*' he repeated in astonishment.

It was difficult for us to realise that he did not recognise our uniforms.

He opened the door wide and then went hobbling to the head of the cellar stairs, where he stood shouting down. There was something very like exultation in the old man's voice. A moment or so later we found ourselves surrounded by women and children, all speaking at once. Even the sergeant made out that they were glad to see us.

One of the younger women asked permission to show us where a Boche machine-gun was situated—in the orchard behind the house. We followed her, creeping along the wall of the house until we came to the corner. Here she pointed to a spot about twenty-five yards away, behind a hedge. We stalked the place, expecting that at any moment the machine-gun would open up. But we reached the spot—only to find that the Boche had left.

From what the peasants told us it appeared that the Germans had cleared out of this house about two hours before we arrived, but were still occupying the further end of the village.

By now our men were coming up in numbers and pushing

forward towards the centre of the village, but it was not till the later afternoon that the Boches were finally pushed out.

The peasants in the house I had first entered and where I now established my company headquarters couldn't do enough for us. Hot coffee, omelettes and bread were shoved in front of us every time we came into the house and when that night Dawson came across to see me the effect of the salute I gave him made a deep impression. Up to the present I had been *Monsieur le commandant*. Now that someone senior to me appeared the whole family stood smartly to attention. The old man, cap in hand, begged permission to perform any service which *Monsieur le Général* might demand. When Dawson instead of sitting down and demanding a meal (which was perhaps what was expected : or maybe they expected something worse) shook hands with each one of them in turn, speaking to them in their own language and (a little self-consciously) patting the children's heads, they were overcome.

It was in this village that I went over a house that had been ransacked by the Germans an hour or so before. The coffee was still hot in the pot out of which they had been drinking. It was a better class house than the others, and had been decently furnished. But now most of the furniture was smashed (presumably to prevent the English from using it) and in one of the bedrooms the contents of a chest of drawers containing mostly lingerie had been strewn over the floor. It was as if burglars had been searching the place for valuables.

The next village we entered (I forget the name of it) was already clear of Germans and as we marched in the inhabitants flocked into the streets to greet us. They brought out glasses of wine and handed them to the troops as they went along. More than once I saw old women drop down on their knees at the side of the road, crossing themselves at the sight of our men.

For the few days that my company occupied this village I was in the position of a military governor. The first thing that happened was that a message was brought to me in my billet—would I receive the wife of the Mayor? She particularly desired to see me. From what I knew of such requests in the villages we had occupied behind the line this meant a request for something or other, or a complaint. I said I would receive her. Her request was not what I had expected.

'Would *Monsieur le Commandant*,' she enquired, 'do the village the great honour of occupying the mayor's house as his headquarters?'

This indeed was something new. Behind the line after four years of occupation the French had learnt to put up with us: but they were always grumbling and certainly none of them had ever *invited* us to occupy their houses.

I thanked the wife of the mayor as best I could and told her that I was quite comfortable where I was and would not trouble her.

So far from troubling her, she persisted, I should be conferring an honour on her household. It was the desire of everyone—and of herself most of all—that *M. le Commandant* should take up his residence with her. What was more, the mayor himself, who was away with his regiment in the south, would wish it. Would I therefore honour her by granting her request? She and her daughters would endeavour to make me as comfortable as possible.

Put that way the request was difficult to refuse and I told Lavender to move my kit at once. The old woman hurried away, delighted. When about half-an-hour later I went along to her house, I found half the village assembled outside waiting to cheer me. Before I went in the aged curé stepped forward and made me what turned out to be a speech of welcome. Though I understood very little of what he said I thanked him in a few ill-chosen words of French and shook hands with him. Everybody clapped. He then put his request, speaking slowly so that I could understand. When the Germans had occupied the village in 1914 they had confiscated all the tricolour flags in the place. But he, the curé, had kept one back. He had cut the red from the white and the white from the blue and had buried the three pieces separately in his cellar, where they still were. Might he now have permission to unearth them, to sew them together again and hoist the tricolour in the village?

When I told him he could go ahead, he lifted his hands as though a miracle had been performed. He had expected, I suppose, that I would take time to consider the proposition, or that I should have to refer it to a higher authority. Perhaps he thought his request would not be granted. At all events it took him some moments to understand that he could hoist the tricolour as soon as he could sew it together. He then burst into tears.

When I went into the house the wife of the mayor was waiting to receive me. Her daughters stood behind her, and they were introduced to me. I was then shown over the house and taken up to the best bedroom. Madame was clearly embarrassed at the modest dimensions of her house and said she hoped that I would not find it too small or inconvenient.

Which, I asked her, was my bedroom?

Madame was astonished. Which other bedroom did I expect to occupy but the best?

'But that,' I said, 'is your bedroom. I would not dream of sleeping here.'

Madame, like the curé, burst into tears. It was clear that under the German occupation she had been treated rather differently. I told her that I was sure that the Mayor would wish her to sleep in her own bedroom. I would take the other bedroom on the same floor. It was smaller and would suit me quite well.

Next morning, when Lavender waked me, he said that the two daughters were quarrelling over which of them should have the honour of polishing my riding boots.

In all the villages we passed through, it was the same thing. People flocking into the streets to cheer us. Some of them dropping down on their knees as we passed. Everyone offering us of their best.

Here is a letter I wrote to my mother describing it all:

We continue to advance. This morning the enemy left one village as we entered it. There is very little fighting.... The inhabitants stand outside the doors, waving to us to come on... As soon as we enter the village everybody cheers, claps, dances, etc., and all the houses put out their long-hidden tricolours. The people beg us to use their houses as billets and do everything in their power to make their 'deliverers' as comfortable as possible. One sees aged women standing at the doorways weeping for joy. They have had Germans with them for four years and they have never seen British troops before, so you can imagine the effect when our infantry, guns, transport, etc., pass through the villages. They all speak of the Germans as 'voleurs', 'cochons', 'brigands', etc. . . . I am at present in command of a village. The inhabitants come and ask me whether they can go about the streets or into other villages—and seem delighted when I tell them that as far as I am concerned they can do what they like! The old man in my billet showed me his permit to go about the village and asked permission to destroy it, which he did with remarkable satisfaction and trampled on the pieces.

In one village I went into a large empty house, looking for billets for my men, and found a blackboard on an easel standing in the middle of the main room. On the blackboard was written in German: 'You are chasing us away now, Tommy, but we shall come back.'

It was in this village that I hurt my leg and was laid up for over a week. I was going the rounds of my company at night when I stepped into an open well. The damage might have been much worse, but it was annoying to be put out of action when so many exciting things were happening. For two days I lay in bed in my billet. Then, as the battalion moved on, there was no alternative but for me to be sent back in an ambulance. I was taken as far as Agnez-les-Duisans, just behind Arras. This was a Casualty Clearing Station and I knew they couldn't keep me there for long. As a matter of fact I spent no more than four hours there and then left hurriedly. Strictly speaking I should have been sent back to the Base to await instructions, but I managed to get by that formality and set out to 'lorry-hop' back to the battalion. It took me a few days to find them because no one I asked could tell me exactly where they were. At last I found them at the little vilalge of Lecelles, north of St. Amand. They were resting there. Other battalions had gone through, carrying on with the advance.

But here was sad news. Dawson had been hit and was in hospital.

It happened this way. He was going his rounds and had just left B Company's headquarters. On his way back he had seen some celery growing in the garden of an empty house and had gone to take some for tea. As he was picking the celery a stray shell came over and fell within a few feet of him, shattering his leg and wounding him in several other places. He managed to slither into a garden shed where he blew his whistle in order to attract attention. It was some time before two men who happened to be passing heard the whistle—and discovered their Colonel.

Dawson was hit on October 23rd by the last shell that was ever fired at our battalion. Incidentally he had been visiting my company's headquarters and I should have been with him, helping him to gather the celery, had it not been for my sprained ankle.

He was taken to Camiers, near Etaples and his parents were sent for. In the last week of November I went to see him in hospital. He was glad—and sorry—to see me. He took it kindly that I had come, but he hated anyone to see him in a helpless state. I stayed with him a little while. Then his lunch was brought. It was a herring and it had to be fed to him by a nurse: but before the meal began he turned me out. He could not have borne to be spoon-fed while I or anybody else (except the nurse) was watching him.

Two weeks later he was dead.

I never knew a man who had a stronger personality, who was more of a born soldier, whose views on aspects of men and affairs I took greater delight in contesting, and whose friendship, which once given was unswerving, evoked a livelier sense of personal loyalty. He was an inspiration to those who served with him and whenever men have spoken of the 6th West Kents they have thought of it as Dawson's battalion.

XXIII

The war ended for us at Lecelles. We never went into action again. On November 11th at 11 a.m. the battalion was drawn up in a square in the tiny village street and a bugler blew the 'Cease Fire'. Three cheers were given for Dawson and for peace. After that the 'Marseillaise' and 'God Save the King' were played. It was not a very impressive ceremony, chiefly I think because we were miles from anywhere and there was no one except ourselves to rejoice with. Also we wished that Dawson could have taken that particular parade. The only incident of the day occurred in the evening when a man in my company, in an effort to shed light (if not learning), shot his arm off with a Very pistol.

The feeling we all had was not one of victory, still less of hatred against the Germans. It was one of relief, coupled with a strong desire to get home.

Naturally rumours began to fly about. Writing from Lecelles on November 14th I told my mother:

I believe that we are here for the duration of the Armistice, but nobody seems to know much of our movements in the future. The general consensus of opinion is that our Division will not go to Germany. Various conjectures are volunteered from various quarters:

(I)   That we shall fill in trenches on the Somme.

(II)   That we shall rebuild houses on Vimy Ridge.

(III) That we shall garrison some Belgian town—possibly Brussels.

(IV)   That the 1st Army will return to England for the ceremonial.

Actually, after a few days the battalion was moved to Auberchicourt, an industrial town whose lack of amenities was equalled only by its ugliness. We spent the time mostly in salvage work, clearing up the mess that the war had left. Sometimes accidents occurred. An old fellow, nearer sixty than fifty, who had joined the battalion a month or so back as a second lieutenant, dropped a shell that he was carrying to the shell-dump and blew himself to pieces. We gave him—or what was left of him—a full-dress military funeral. It was a sad affair, but it gave the troops something to do, learning the ceremonial.

It was at Auberchicourt that A Company mutinied. They refused to come on parade saying that their boots weren't fit to wear, which was pretty true. While the war was on they would not have dreamed of mutinying. Now that the war was over and the danger past they began to think of themselves and what was due to them. They could scarcely be blamed. They were still, like most of us, not soldiers but civilians in uniform.

In December I took a day off in order to revisit the Cambrai battlefield.

> The whole battlefield [I wrote to my mother] is deserted, the only signs of life are the birds, especially the partridges, which are very plentiful at this time of year. Gilbert's grave is in a very quiet spot. The strip of metal with his name on it which was placed there in November 1917, to mark the spot, is still there. We are having crosses put up. I went down the dug-out which was Brigade H.Q. and saw the place where I slept, but my Sam Browne and haversack were no longer there.*

Auberchicourt was a dreary place. Harry Barnard was put in charge of it. I was glad of his companionship. When Christmas came we did our best to paint the place red for the sake of the men and for our own sakes as well. But our minds were not on the battalion any more. We were thinking all the time of England and of how soon we were going to get there.

My own thoughts were turned towards Cambridge. I had no wish to remain in the Army and now that Dawson was dead no question arose of my doing so. It is true that one day I was sent for and asked if I would care to be made Staff Captain of another Brigade in the Division. I even went to lunch with the General of that Brigade. But nothing came of the idea. On January 26th, 1919, I left Auberchicourt and returned to England.

XXIV

What did we thing of it all? I have said that when the Armistice was signed what we chiefly felt was relief. I think that feeling was general. It has often been declared that the men who fought in the Great War fought to end all wars, fought to make the

---

* In September 1938 I went there again with my wife and elder son. The British cemetery where Gilbert, Alderman and the others had finally been buried lay a mile or so from where they had been killed. The entrance to the dug-out which had been our Brigade headquarters was still visible—in the middle of a cornfield—and the shaft was cluttered up with old rifles and tin helmets.

world safe for democracy, fought for the establishment of the League of Nations. Idealism underlay the conception of the cause for which we were fighting and the morality of our position was doubted no more than was our capacity to win. But in my experience very few of the men who fought had a clear view of the constructive aims for which we were at war. I don't think I ever heard the phrases 'war to end war', 'a world safe for democracy', and 'the League of Nations' used until after the war was over. I don't mean that public men didn't use them in speeches. I mean that the great majority of men at the front didn't use them or even think of using them. If you had asked the average Tommy or company officer what he thought he was fighting for, the reply would have been 'to beat the Boche'.

That does not imply that many of us, when the war was over, did not expect some better system of regulating international affairs. We did. We also held a strong conviction, a certainty with most of us, that never again in our lifetime would war be allowed to break out. I remember a friend of mine, about the year 1922, telling me in astonishment that he had heard someone talking about 'the next war'. The next war! We roared with laughter. The fellow clearly must have been a lunatic—we thought.

In pre-1914 days foreign policy was commonly regarded as a matter for experts, for the close corporation of the Foreign Office and the Diplomatic Service. Perhaps it was natural that after the Armistice all most of us thought about was returning to civilian life and getting on with whatever job awaited us.

In my case it was Cambridge. A week after leaving Auberchicourt I was sitting at the Freshmen's table at Clare. Next to me was a colonel, also a Freshman, one of whose subalterns, being a Fellow of the College, was seated at High Table.